THE

Spirituality

OF

Fasting

The range and depth of this little book are impressive! Msgr. Charles Murphy presents a comprehensive history of fasting and offers a sound rationale for the need to revive this ancient practice. A must-read for any serious Christian and a wonderful resource for adult faith formation, small faith communities, or parish social justice committees.

Susan Lang Abbott
Director of Religious Education
Archdiocese of Boston

Msgr. Charles M. Murphy, an experienced pastor and theologian, takes a fresh look at the neglected Christian practice of fasting. Brilliant and readable . . . the book is a perfect example of retrieving an ancient Christian practice for modern people.

Rev. Richard Clifford, S.J.
Dean, Boston College School of Theology and Ministry

The Spirituality of Fasting articulates what St. Augustine meant when he wrote, "Longing deepens the heart." Religious fasting, devoted to prayer and charity, can "transform our total being, mind, body, and spirit," and can strengthen the Christian community.

Margaret R. Miles
Emerita Professor of Historical Theology
Graduate Theological Union, Berkeley

For those of us seriously seeking to renew our spiritual lives, Msgr. Murphy's comprehensive book gives a deeply helpful understanding of the indispensable rediscovery of fasting as a pillar of our faith and an integral part of our lifelong quest for the Lord Jesus.

Msgr. Peter J. Vaghi
Author of *The Faith We Profess*

This eloquent, historically enlightening, and practical guide to a Catholic and religious understanding of fasting motivates us to take a new look at an old virtue. Must reading for anyone serious about finding the only real food that can quench their hunger and thirst for God and for growing in compassion and greater charity.

Walter E. Grazer
Author of *Catholics Going Green*

This reader-friendly text, sensitive to holistic emphases in contemporary spirituality, anchors in the Bible and the formative centuries of Christian life a still valuable but now neglected practice. Msgr. Charles Murphy's treatment of fasting makes a very positive contribution towards shoring up the three traditional pillars of Judaeo-Christian piety—prayer, fasting, works of charity—in harmonious relation to one another.

Rev. Thomas Ryan, C.S.P.
Author of *Fasting Rediscovered*

THE
Spirituality
OF
Fasting

Rediscovering a Christian Practice

Charles M. Murphy

ave maria press AmP notre dame, indiana

© 2010 by Ave Maria Press, Inc.

Founded in 1865, Ave Maria Press is a ministry of the Indiana Province of Holy Cross.

www.avemariapress.com

ISBN-10 1-59471-243-3 ISBN-13 978-1-59471-243-2

Cover and text design by Brian C. Conley.

Cover image © 2009 Jupiterimages Corporation

Printed and bound in the United States of America.

for

William Cardinal Levada

Prefect, Congregation for the Doctrine of the Faith,

Classmate and Friend, on the Occasion of the

Twenty-fifth Anniversary of His Episcopal Ordination

Contents

Preface

This is a book about the religious discipline of fasting, its theory and practice. Food in a time of plenty and easy access to it have become major preoccupations for everyone. Advice abounds about proper diets and regimes to lose weight. Although these concerns are important, my book has a different focus and purpose. For a variety of reasons that I will explore, religious fasting has drastically declined among Roman Catholics and many other Christians. My aim is to make it once more a central act of piety, but on a more solid basis than in the recent past. I want to show its roots in scripture and tradition, and liberate it from legalisms that obscured its true meaning.

This is how I define the religious practice of fasting, sharply delineating it from dieting and medically supervised fasts: religious fasting first of all is an act of humility before God, a penitential expression of our need for conversion from sin and selfishness. Its aim is nothing less than helping us to become more loving persons, loving God above all and our neighbor as ourselves. Its purpose therefore is the transformation of our total being—mind, body, and spirit. Fasting cannot achieve these aims unless its focus is on God in prayer and not on ourselves. For this reason, fasting takes place at appropriate times within the liturgical year whose centerpiece is Easter. Fasting reaches its crescendo during the forty days of Lent, the immediate preparation for the celebration of the Easter mysteries. As such, it is a necessary implementation of our baptismal promises to live in the freedom of God's adopted children. Fasting realizes its goal when we share fully in Christ's passage from death to life. We then enter into the "today" of Easter which, for Christians, is no mere past event but an entirely new level of existence in our present life. And we experience this "today" together as we engage in fasting together at times designated in our tradition. Fasting finds its most powerful expression as a corporate exercise within the Body of Christ.

I wish to thank Father John Custer, one of my former students, and former dean of the Byzantine Catholic Seminary of Saints Cyril and Methodius in Pittsburgh, for his contributions to this book. I am also indebted to Kate O'Halloran and to Charles Skriner for their editorial assistance. Father Custer, when he was a seminarian during my rectorship of the North American College, Vatican City, told me that the book by the Russian Orthodox theologian, Alexander Schmemann, *Great Lent: Journey to Pascha*, introduced him and his generation to the meaning of fasting.[1] My hope is that this book may do something of the same for the present generation of Catholics.

INTRODUCTION:

The Loss *of a* Tradition

"What happened to fast and abstinence in the Church in the United States?" Pope John Paul II asked me this question over dinner when we sat together in the refectory of the North American College in Rome on February 22, 1980. The Holy Father, soon after his election as pope, had visited the United States and evidently was surprised by what he perceived to be the collapse of these venerable practices. Such a change was especially noteworthy among American Catholics, who were brought up to believe that Church laws regarding fast and abstinence were serious obligations and their infraction was a mortal sin. Looking around a restaurant on any Friday in America, for instance, you could almost tell who the Catholics were by what they had on their plates. Fish on Friday and fasting during Lent and before major feasts created a whole rhythm of life among Catholics, even in countries where the laws were less strictly observed.

Special cuisines such as the "supper of the seven fishes" on Christmas Eve in Italy were created to accommodate these rules.

One event that precipitated such momentous change throughout the world can be dated, February 17, 1966, when Pope Paul VI issued the apostolic constitution on fast and abstinence, *Poenitemini*. The clear intent of the document, in keeping with the spiritual renewal undertaken by the Second Vatican Council, was to rescue fasting from the legalism and minimalism into which it had fallen. While this document paid tribute to the ancient penitential practices, it asserted that they did not fit easily into the circumstances in which people live today. It suggested that the practice of the virtue of penance today could be translated, for example, into faithfulness to our occupational duties, acceptance of the vexations that accompany our work environment every day, and patient enduring of the trials of modern life with all its insecurities, in addition to the traditional practices.[1] The constitution goes on to recommend voluntary, self-chosen penances such as works of charity on behalf of the poor as complements to or even substitutes for fasting. The old custom of "giving things up" for Lent thus became disparaged as something negative, while "doing things for others" was seen as more positive.

In keeping with this new approach, the Mass prayers for Lent underwent change. While the old Prefaces to the Eucharistic Prayer stressed fasting and penance and their benefits, the new prayers also emphasized deeds of charity and other virtuous acts as good preparations for the reception of Easter joy. The character of Lent thereby was given a somewhat different focus.

Another development in the Church growing out of the reforms of the Second Vatican Council also affected the way Catholics came to regard Church laws in themselves. In the council's decree on priestly formation, a new approach to moral theology was envisioned, more biblically based and positive in outlook, freed of the legalism of the past.[2] Before the council, moral theology had become an offshoot of canon law. When canon law, for example, stated that the Church's laws regarding fast and abstinence from meat were of "serious obligation," moralists translated this to mean that any conscious violation meant that a "mortal sin" had been incurred. These are, however, different categories, morally speaking, and the effect was that the ancient religious tradition regarding fast and abstinence became cast in legalism and negativity. The moral theology after the council rightly sought to overcome this legalism, but it had the unexpected consequence of bringing about a greatly reduced estimation and practice of these essential religious obligations.

A striking example of the old mentality was given me by a priest who described his deceased grandmother as a true expert in matters of fast and abstinence. Although, he said, she considered herself to be a faithful Catholic, she boasted of the fact that she had never fasted in her entire life. At a young age she married a laboring man and, according to canon law, a laboring man and his family were exempted from the laws of fasting because of the rigorous nature of his work. The grandmother was over the age of sixty when her husband died and so once again, according to Church law, she was exempt. The grandmother's conclusion, the priest stated, was that fasting was something made up by the bishops and had nothing at all to do with Jesus! The legalism around fasting in which she had been reared prevented her from seeing its religious value for herself.

In this book I propose a renewal of the practice of fast and abstinence based upon a deeper understanding of its role in our religious life. Prayer, fasting, and charity, as we will see, are the three pillars of Old Testament piety that were taken over and confirmed in the New Testament. In the Book of Tobit, a classic text of Jewish piety, we read, "Prayer with fasting and alms with uprightness are better than riches with iniquity" (Tb 12:8). Jesus in his foundational sermon on discipleship, the Sermon on the Mount in St. Matthew's Gospel, made specific reference to these pillars as part of the greater righteousness to which he was calling his followers (Mt 6:1–18). By his personal example of fasting forty days, Jesus laid the foundations for what would become for the whole Church the communal preparation for the celebration of Easter, the Christian feast of feasts (Mt 4:1–11; Lk 4:1–13).

The first charge given in the gospels by Jesus to his disciples is, "Repent and believe the gospel!" (Mk 1:15). This is why the obligations to pray, fast, and do works of charity are so central. They are the most important means to accomplish our repentance, our turning away (literally, "conversion") from sinfulness. As the *Catechism of the Catholic Church* teaches through fasting, our conversion is directed to ourselves; through prayer, our conversion focuses us upon God; and through almsgiving, our conversion expresses itself in compassionate concern for our neighbor.[3]

The Body Is the Soul's Workshop

As we will see later in this book, the ascetics who lived the Christian life in the Egyptian desert in the fourth and fifth centuries, through their witness and teachings, have given us great wisdom about the necessity of fast and abstinence in our lives. They became convinced that the condition of the body reflects the condition of the soul. An undisciplined body reveals an undisciplined soul. Body and soul have a reciprocal influence upon each other because they are dimensions of each person's identity. These desert fathers also became aware, by the deep soul work in which they engaged in their solitary existence, that the achievement of purity of heart and the capacity to practice divine charity required control of the unruly self and all its desires.

To achieve these goals, fasting is as essential now as it was then. For other reasons people today recognize the need to pay more attention to our bodies. Hermitages were popular then; now it's health spas, gyms, and physical fitness clubs, where guidance and coaching are provided by trainers performing roles similar to the spiritual directors of the past. But like the early Christian practitioners, we know we have to look deeply within ourselves in order to achieve better balance and greater happiness. Just as there is no substitute for working out in the gym in order to train the body, so there is no substitute for fasting—for example, by doing works of charity—in order to achieve the purity of heart that we seek. The ancients, we realize, were correct in their conviction that prayer and fasting are needed if true charity, unhindered by our selfishness, is to take place at all.

The Second Vatican Council (1962–65) was the first ecumenical council to give specific attention to lay Christians and their specific vocation as disciples of Christ. The council declared that

> all the faithful of Christ of whatever rank or status are called to the fullness of the Christian life and to the perfection of charity. . . . In the various types and duties of life, one and the same holiness is cultivated by all who are moved by the Spirit of God and who obey the voice of the Father, worshiping God the Father in spirit and in truth."[4]

In Catholicism, therefore, there is no such thing as "second-class citizenship," with monks pursuing perfection and everyone else confined to more earthly pursuits. What is often forgotten, however, is that the ascetic practices developed by the monks in accordance with scripture must find a place in every life if the same perfection is to be achieved. Lent in fact had its origin, in part, in the desire to make monastic asceticism part of every Christian's life.

In her introduction to Patrick Leigh Fermor's classic book on monasticism, *A Time to Keep Silence,* Karen Armstrong describes how the Benedictine monks of Cluny, near Paris, carried out evangelization in the eleventh century—not by mere catechetical instruction, which does not automatically bring with it a conversion of life, but by an experience, limited and for a time, of monastic rigors. Even a limited experience of the monastic life can introduce people to the real meaning of religion far more effectively than abstract theological beliefs. Thus the monks of Cluny, in their effort to educate the laity of Europe, sent them on pilgrimage, which, under the aegis of Cluny, became a hugely popular activity. While they traveled to their holy destination—to Rome, Compostella, or a local shrine—laymen and laywomen had to live for a time like monks. The pilgrims turned their backs on their normal lives and lived a communal life; they prayed together, they were celibate for the duration of the pilgrimage, and they were forbidden to fight or bear arms. Moreover, the hardships of the journey were experienced as a form of asceticism. In all, the experience was designed to transform their behavior in such a way that they would come to know the deeper meaning of Christian faith.[5]

In my two visits to Buddhist lands, I was impressed with how many laypeople were proud to tell us about the periods of time they spent in monastic training. For us Westerners, "temporary" monasticism is not known as such, but perhaps there is much wisdom in this practice as the monks of Cluny demonstrated by their popular pilgrimages.

Another good effect of a revival of fast and abstinence in the Church would be the reassertion of religious identity among Catholics. Leaving much up to individual choice and personal preference in our penitential practices has the tendency to deprive us of the group élan and mutual encouragement so necessary in religious life and so basic to human life in general. In a recent study reported in the *New England Journal of Medicine*, obesity was found to spread like a virus from person to person, especially among friends, family members, and sometimes neighbors. Doing things together, so much a part of being human, has huge effects, both positive and negative. The greatest religious phenomenon in the world today is Ramadan, during which millions of people all over the world, together, publicly fast and pray. Basketball fans will always remember the example of Hakeem Olajuwon, who starred in the playoffs for the Houston Rockets in 2006 and did so while fasting during the month of Ramadan.

How much our secularized world needs such demonstrations of religious practice and personal sacrifice.

Our National Eating Disorder

In a much-read and -discussed book, *The Omnivore's Dilemma: A Natural History of Four Meals,* Michael Pollan describes what he diagnoses as "our national eating disorder." He attributes this condition to something missing in contemporary America, namely, deeply rooted traditions surrounding food and eating.[6] Pollan describes eating as not only a biological act, but also one that is ecological and political in its meaning and consequence. I would add that eating is also something more—a religious act that celebrates our deepest ties to God, the earth, and one another. Thinking of eating in this way helps us realize how greatly reduced and less satisfying eating has become when it is nothing more than a refueling exercise engaged in alone and on the run.

Our national eating disorder explains how dieting has replaced fasting for many people. People diet, of course, in order to achieve better health. Often, however, dieting becomes an obsession if individuals have absorbed cultural models of beauty and attractiveness that are inhuman and oppressive and that cause them to hate themselves and their bodies. News reports in the early years of this century about six aspiring young models from Brazil who within a six-month period starved themselves to death do not surprise us. No wonder in Milan and Madrid women who are overly thin have been banned from participation in fashion shows, as they are considered dangerous role models. The psychological problems of anorexia and bulimia are very complex and difficult to treat. For persons so suffering, the notion of being overweight becomes something horrific and repulsive. In this regard Aelred Squire, a scholar of early Church history, has made this helpful observation:

> It may well be thought that Western man in particular has reached such a degree of psychological alienation from his body that to help him to fast and to mortify his bodily life without helping him to change his attitude towards it is to try to push him further in the direction which, if left to himself, he must in the end inevitably accomplish his own destruction.[7]

In October 2005 the Australian musician Keith Urban entered the Betty Ford rehabilitation center in California. There was no one large crisis, he explained, but a lot of small things that together made his life "unmanageable." Urban said he found the regime of recovery at the center so helpful that he remained there ninety days instead of the usual thirty. What he received was not merely assistance in giving up unhealthy habits, but new insights about how to live. As he put it, "Abstinence was one thing, but there was all this other area of my life to start learning about." He concluded with this observation: "Abstinence is the ticket into the movie, it is not the movie."[8]

The July 16, 2007, issue of *Time* magazine had as its cover story, "How We Get Addicted: New brain research is helping us understand why we get hooked—and how we may get cured." Its author, Michael D. Lemonick, argued that the solution to addiction is not something like Alcoholics Anonymous, which Lemonick dismisses as non-professional and unscientific, but rather new designer drugs that show promise in cutting off the craving that drives an addict toward relapse. What these drugs do is change the chemistry of the brain and repair previous brain damage.

In my view this is but another instance, so common in our day, of the attempt to use drugs to treat illness and avoid the difficult task of treating the person who has the illness. Addiction often is not merely a chemical problem but also a spiritual one. Alcoholics Anonymous (AA) recognizes this truth in its own "unscientific" way, using what the article describes as "folk wisdom." AA confronts the person who is addicted and requires the person's active involvement in the cure. It also provides the personal support that is crucial in the ninety days of recovery when the brain can re-set itself. The spiritual gains in the AA approach are many and life-shaping: personal responsibility, mending relationships, acceptance of support from others and, even more critically, the fervent petition for divine grace to overcome the power of the addiction which human willpower alone cannot achieve.

In this book it is my intention to re-introduce Catholics and others to the life-enhancing practices of fasting and abstinence, and to the vision of life upon which these are based. Abstinence and dieting alone are merely "tickets into the movie," as Keith Urban helpfully observed; they are not the movie itself—our life as we must live it. Jesus declared, "I have come so that they may have life and have it to the full" (Jn 10:10). Fasting and abstinence are part of this greater life that God intends for all of us.

Recovering the Christian Practice of Fasting

In 1983 Joseph Ratzinger, later Pope Benedict XVI, was invited to give the Lenten retreat to the pope and his curia at the Vatican. I found his reflections on the first Sunday of Lent to be particularly sharp and beneficial:

> Jesus' road begins with the forty days of fasting, as did those of Moses and Elijah. Jesus told the disciples that a certain kind of demon is not to be cast out in any other way than by prayer and fasting. Cardinal Willebrands [Cardinal Johannes Willebrands at that time was president of the Pontifical Council for Promoting Christian Unity] told me that after the talks with the [Coptic Church], their patriarch in Egypt said that at the end of his visit to Rome, "Yes, I have understood that our faith in Jesus Christ, true God and true man, is identical. But I have found that the Church of Rome has abolished fasting and without fasting there is no church."
>
> The primacy of God is not really achieved if it does not also include man's corporality. The truly central actions of man's biological life are eating and reproduction, sensuality. Therefore virginity and fasting have been from the beginning of the Christian tradition two indispensable expressions of the primacy of God, of faith in the reality of God. Without being given corporal expression also, the primacy of God with difficulty remains of decisive moment in man's life. It is true that fasting is not all there is to Lent, but it is something indispensable for which there is no substitute. Freedom in the actual application of fasting is good and corresponds to the different situations in which we find ourselves. But a communal and public act of the Church seems to be no less necessary than in past times, as a public testimony to the primacy of God and of spiritual values, as much as solidarity with all who are starving. Without fasting we shall in no way cast out the demon of our time.[9]

These words of the future Pope Benedict XVI provide an excellent summary of the themes of this book.

The chapters of this book strive to show the profound connection between body and soul illuminated by the practice of fasting. In the first chapter, I provide a brief history of fasting in the Church, as well as an overview of its contemporary practice in the Western and Eastern churches. In the second chapter we explore the practice of fasting in the scriptures. The next two chapters describe the crucial role of fasting in the achievement of humility before God, the overcoming of our selfishness and unruly desires, and the personal discipline required to prepare our bodies for their glorious transformation by the power of Christ's resurrection. The fifth chapter shows the profound links between charity and fasting as they manifest themselves in a type of fasting that takes into account the most impoverished and vulnerable among us. In chapter 6 we will propose a program of fasting and prayer that incorporates the values we strive to honor in our earthly journey to God. Finally, because this book is intended not only to help readers theologically reflect on fasting, but also to practice it in their own lives, at the end of each chapter I include suggestions for reflection that are meant to help lead to such practice.

CHAPTER 1:

Recovering *a* Tradition

St. Elizabeth Ann Seton (1774–1821) was the first native-born American citizen to be canonized a saint. Raised an Episcopalian, she lost her husband at a young age, leaving her with five children. Elizabeth was befriended in her bereavement by an Italian family in Livorno, the place where her husband died during their visit to Europe. It was in part the deep and abiding impression this family made upon her that led Elizabeth to embrace Catholicism. Along with Bishop John Carroll, Elizabeth Seton is considered to have co-founded the Church in the United States.

A great part of her favorable impression of Catholicism came from her observation of the Catholic family's observance of Lent and of fasting in particular. Writing from Italy to her soul sister Rebecca, she says:

You may remember when I asked Mr. H [Rev. John Henry Hobart, curate at Trinity Episcopal Church, New York City] what was meant by fasting in our prayer book—as I found myself on Ash Wednesday morning saying so foolishly to God, "I turn to you in fasting, weeping and mourning," and I had come to church with a hearty breakfast of buckwheat cakes and coffee, and full of life and spirits, with little thought of my sins—you may remember what he said about its being old customs, etc. Well, the dear Mrs. F. [Filicchi, her Catholic host in Livorno] who I am with, never eats, the season of Lent, till after the clock strikes three. Then the family assembles. And she says she offers her weakness and pain of fasting for her sins, united with Our Savior's sufferings. I like that very much.[1]

This of course is precisely what has largely passed out of popular Catholic practice in recent years. It is understandable that Pope John Paul II, when he dined with us at the North American College, would raise this as a question.

As it happened it was in the season of Lent that his visit took place. While we were still contemplating what kind of a meal to serve the pope, word came from the Vatican that the pope wanted to dine only on soup and bread. We thus caught a glimpse of how the pope himself was fasting in Lent and how personal was the question he posed during that meal about what had happened to fasting and abstinence in our country. But how to bring them back? In a way, this book is my response to that question, which I have lived with these many years.

A Brief History of
Lent and the Practice of Fasting

> Father, you have taught us to overcome our sins by prayer,
> fasting, and works of mercy. When we are discouraged by
> our weakness, give us confidence in your love.

The above is the gathering prayer for the Mass of the
Third Sunday of Lent. With the typical austerity and simplicity of the Roman Rite, it joins together the three biblical practices that are the foundation stones not only of this
annual season of repentance but of the entire Christian life:
prayer, fasting, and works of mercy. When this prayer was
composed, the Roman liturgy was passing from its Greek or-
igins into its final Latin form. It was during this period, from
approximately the third to the sixth centuries, that Lent as a
forty-day period preparing for Easter came into being.

Lent evolved as a way that the whole body of believers
could participate in the ascetical practices modeled by the
heroic monks and hermits of the centuries before. The early desert fathers did not consider themselves anything more
than average Christians who were striving to put into practice the teachings of Christ. They were close to the time when
being a Christian meant willingness to suffer the loss of your
life for your faith. Many of them conceived of their daily
life as the opportunity to experience a spiritual martyrdom.
Lent made it practical and possible for everyone, to some degree, to learn and to practice the asceticism required by the
gospel.

Lent did not begin as a forty-day observance, however.
In the East at the time of the desert fathers, with the excep-
tion of the festive fifty days between Easter and Pentecost,

all Christians were expected to fast every Wednesday and Friday. Wednesday was a day of penance because it was believed that on that day Judas betrayed the Lord, and Friday was commemorated as the day of the Lord's death. In the West, until about the fourth century, fasting was not something done communally; it was something that some individuals chose to do. It became more generalized when the custom arose of the community of the faithful joining candidates for baptism in their penitential practices during their six weeks of preparation for reception into the Church at Easter. By the seventh century the Lenten observances were extended as they are today to Ash Wednesday.[2] It should also be noted that Holy Thursday was the traditional day for the granting of sacramental absolution of sins after an extended period of public penance. Although not originally associated with Lent, penitential practices during this time before Easter were therefore common.

In the early centuries a devotion also grew up around the forty hours Jesus spent in the tomb. It took the form of fasting, prayers, and acts of contrition. Scholars have noted that the very encapsulated symbol of faith, the Apostles' Creed, says not just that Jesus died, but that "he died and was buried." It was the source of pious amazement that the Son of God had subjected himself to this much voluntary humiliation. Fasting became one way of expressing that amazement.[3] This minor episode in the history of fasting resonates with an experience of my own. As a newly ordained priest I spent a day in prayer at Mount Calvary and next to the Holy Sepulcher in Jerusalem. The day passed without my realizing it. It was suddenly evening and I realized I had not eaten a thing or even thought about food.

Over the centuries, however, fasting became more and more removed from the vital practice exemplified by the desert ascetics, and the practice began to take on the shape of Church legislation. We can begin to see this in what St. Thomas Aquinas (1225–74) has to say on the subject of fasting, as he summarizes Church legislation about what is to be eaten: only one full meal on days of partial fasting, to be taken between noon and three in the afternoon, and no meat, milk from mammals, or eggs from birds during Lent.[4] Over time these rules became more complex and detailed, with exceptions and exemptions being drawn, as the example of the priest's grandmother in the introductory chapter illustrated.

Aquinas lists three motives for fasting, all biblically based. First, fasting is the guardian of chastity, as the Apostle Paul teaches (2 Cor 6:5). Second, fasting helps our minds rise more freely to the heights of contemplation, as was the case with the prophet Daniel who, after fasting for three weeks, was granted a divine revelation (Dn 10:3). Third, fasting is a penitential practice by which we can make satisfaction for sin, as Joel the prophet instructed us (Jl 2:12). As for times that are appropriate for fasting, Aquinas singles out the period before Easter as preeminent and also takes note of the seasonal Ember Days.[5] Despite the biblical basis for this treatment of fasting, it is noteworthy that Aquinas places fasting in the context of the natural virtue of temperance. In this, Aquinas seems to draw inspiration more from Aristotle than from the biblical triad of prayer, fasting, and charity, perhaps an early sign of the decline in the spiritual basis of fasting that would occur over the following centuries.

The Current Church Practice of Fasting

As Alexander Schmemann explains in his book *Great Lent: Journey to Pascha*, there are two types of Church fasting: total and partial. Total fasting involves a complete renunciation of all food and drink, sometimes including even the renunciation of water. It obviously is of limited duration. Partial fasting, on the other hand, is to be practiced for an extensive period. This type of fasting involves a reduction in the amount of food taken over the course of the day, according to certain guidelines.

The two types of fasting have different purposes. Total fasting from all food and drink has as its purpose to produce a true feeling of bodily hunger which is to help us uncover our deep spiritual hunger for God. It is to allow us to adopt our true spiritual posture in relationship to God: complete humility, vulnerability, and helplessness. Partial fasting must be practiced for an extended period because our spiritual healing from the effects of our sinful life requires a greater length to be accomplished as our bodies, minds, and spirits strive to reset themselves. Partial fasting is also called ascetical fasting. Our hearts of stone become transformed to hearts of flesh, as the scriptures put it, hearts capable of feeling and compassion.[6]

As Father Schmemann explains, Lent is the great season for ascetical fasting, although there are other times in the year when total and partial fasting are prescribed. Lent, he says, is misunderstood if we think of it as a time when good things are forbidden. "Lent is exactly the opposite; it is a return to the 'normal' life, to that fasting that Adam and Eve broke, thus introducing suffering and death into the world.

Lent is greeted, therefore, as a spiritual spring, as a true joy and light."[7]

Total fast is most often associated with the Eucharist, the reception of the Body and Blood of the Lord. In ancient times and in Orthodoxy today, the Eucharistic fast is prolonged, but in Catholic practice it has been reduced to one hour before the time of reception.

Let us take a closer look at these two types of fast, as they are practiced today in the Roman Catholic and Eastern Orthodox traditions.

ROMAN CATHOLIC TRADITIONS

Total Fast

In Roman Catholic canon law, total fast from all food and drink except water is prescribed as a preparation for the reception of the Eucharist for at least an hour beforehand. In the previous code of canon law, a communicant was to fast from midnight before receiving Holy Communion. In the past also total fasts were to be observed before major feasts — Easter, Pentecost, and Christmas, among others. Total fast could profitably be reintroduced on these occasions and others so that a crucial element of fasting, a true hunger for God in body and soul, may once again become part of Christian life.

Partial Fast

Partial fast is penitential in nature. In the Church calendar, the most penitential season is Lent, as we approach the time when Jesus sacrificed himself for us. Penitential fasting is thus required on the days that mark the beginning of Lent and the day of the Lord's death — Ash Wednesday and Good

Friday. In the past, as noted above, partial fasting was to be observed on all the Wednesdays and Fridays of the year, as well as abstinence from meat. According to contemporary canon law, partial fasting requires taking no more than one full meal a day supplemented by two smaller ones (or snacks) which together are not to equal the size of the main meal. This law applies to those between the ages of eighteen and fifty-eight.

In addition to the Lenten season, in former times partial fasts were to be observed seasonally on days called "Ember Days," which were linked with the agricultural calendar and were united with prayers for good crops. Ember Days were observed four times a year on Wednesdays, Fridays, and Saturdays. In 2003, the U.S. Bishops' Committee on Divine Worship recommended a recovery of the practice of Ember Days:

> In many rural dioceses, days are already set aside for asking God's blessing on the harvest, the granting of sufficient rain and a general protection against storms. However, the notion of an "Ember Day" may be understood from a broader perspective. . . . In line with their specific needs, dioceses might then set aside one day in each season (with or without fast and abstinence) and encourage special intentions to be prayed for accordingly. In this way, the many and varied needs of the Church can be addressed flexibly and practically.[8]

A renewed practice might also mean a return to partial fasting every day during the season of Lent as well as abstinence from meat. Today, abstinence from meat is required—for everyone between the ages of fourteen and fifty-nine—on Ash Wednesday and Good Friday as well as on all the Fridays of Lent, unless the local bishops' conferences allow the substitution of other forms of penance personally chosen. As noted above, prior to Vatican II such abstinence was required on all Fridays of the year. In their 1966 pastoral statement on fasting and abstinence, the bishops of the United States recommended that Catholics continue this weekly abstinence, now of their own free will rather than under obligation. In that statement the bishops explained the special religious significance of Friday as a penitential day throughout the year.

> Friday itself remains a special day of penitential observance throughout the year. . . . Friday should be in each week something of what Lent is in the entire year. For this reason we urge all to prepare for that weekly Easter that comes each Sunday by freely making of each Friday a day of self-denial and mortification in prayerful remembrance of the passion of Jesus Christ.
>
> Among the works of voluntary self-denial and personal penance which we especially recommend to our people . . . we give first place to abstinence from flesh meat. We do so in the hope that the Catholic community will ordinarily continue to abstain from meat by free choice as formerly we did in obedience to Church law. . . . Our deliberate personal abstinence from meat, more especially because no longer required by law, will be an outward sign of inward spiritual values that we cherish. . . .
>
> Fridays will acquire among us other forms of penitential witness which may become as much a part of the devout way of life in the future as Friday abstinence from meat. . . . It would bring great glory to God and good to souls if Fridays found our people doing volunteer work in hospitals, visiting the sick, serving the needs of the aged and lonely, instructing the young in the faith, participating

as Christians in community affairs, and meeting our obligations to our families, our friends, our neighbors, and our communities, including our parishes, with a special zeal born of a living faith.

Let it be proved by the spirit in which we enter upon prayer and penance, not excluding fast and abstinence freely chosen, that these present decisions and recommendations of this conference of bishops will herald a new birth of loving faith and a more profound penitential conversion, by both of which we become one with Christ, mature sons and daughters of God, and servants of God's people.[9]

ORTHODOX AND BYZANTINE CATHOLIC TRADITIONS

Total Fast

The East like the West associates total fast with eucharistic preparation. The presence of the Lord in this great sacrament is the occasion for unusual celebration and feasting. The Sundays of the year therefore are not fasting days. On Saturdays, however, many engage in a total fast—the length of which varies greatly from congregation to congregation—before reception of communion at the Sunday liturgy.

Partial Fast

In the Orthodox calendar there are four periods of partial fasting: the seasons before Easter, Christmas, the feast of Saints Peter and Paul (June 29), and the Dormition of the Blessed Virgin Mary (August 15).

The Wednesdays and Fridays of Lent are times when no food may be taken until after sunset. Two Sundays before the start of Lent, abstinence from meat begins and lasts through the whole season ("Meat-Fare Sunday"). On the Sunday before Ash Wednesday ("Cheese-Fare Sunday"), dairy products and eggs are removed from the diet until Easter.

Diet and cuisine obviously are cultural phenomena, strongly influenced by history and geography. One outstanding feature of Byzantine fasting is abstinence from luxury products, specifically wine and olive oil, in the original Mediterranean milieu. On the other hand, while Byzantine traditions prohibit both meat and fish during prescribed times, they do not include abstinence from shellfish, which were plentiful and cheap and were considered more like insects than animals. A parishioner in a Byzantine Catholic parish in the United States, upon hearing these rules, commented to the pastor, "So, Father, you are saying I can live on Scotch and lobster for forty days? Count me in!" Of course he could not if he truly understood the thrust of these rules which is a greater simplicity and austerity during this holy season.

A distinctively Byzantine custom, derived from the practice of the first desert ascetics, is what is called "dry eating": a Lenten diet consisting of fruits and vegetables that can be eaten either raw or just boiled. This means that olive oil is forbidden either as a cooking medium or a condiment. This healthy regime fits nicely with the ascetical aims of Lent.

Ecumenical Witness

In March 2007 I sat down in Rome with Cardinal Walter Kasper, president of the Secretariat for Christian Unity, and explored the question of the very different practices of fasting in the Orthodox and Roman churches, and particularly the fact that fasting in the Roman Catholic Church has shrunk to minimum proportions. I asked if the disparity in fasting practices had come up in the dialogues with the Orthodox which have become such an important priority for the Church. I recalled the joint declaration of Pope Paul VI and the Orthodox pope of Alexandria, Shenouda III, which stressed the common heritage of the Orthodox and Catholics, and which highlighted the statement, "We keep the fasts and feasts of our faith."[10] Moreover, Pope John Paul II once proposed that it would be highly desirable that Roman Catholic and Orthodox Christians decide on a common date for the celebration of our central feast of Easter. Such a common witness united with intensified fasting and abstinence during Lent would be fitting expressions of our common faith and our shared religious heritage.

Cardinal Kasper said there has not been a recent discussion of fasting on this level, but he did make the following observations. He does not believe there should be a new papal document such as *Poenitemini* legislating from the top a return to the ancient practices. Instead, he mused, the way it can happen is from local congregations, dioceses, and even individuals deciding to re-commit themselves to restore emphasis upon these religious observances which have proven so effective in living the Christian life and are part of the gospel itself. Perhaps, in this endeavor, Catholics might partner with their Orthodox brothers and sisters in giving a common witness. This actually is more in keeping with the spirit of fasting and abstinence as these are observed by Orthodox Christians even today. It is not by means of legislation but by mutual encouragement and support that people decide to engage in these practices. This was certainly true for the Eastern-rite seminarians I knew as rector: they joined fellow seminarians in committing themselves to a faithful program of renewed asceticism without anyone telling them to do so. It would be entirely appropriate, for example, at the start of Lent, for a family to decide among themselves how in their particular Christian household they would observe together the ancient practices of fasting from food and abstinence from meat.

POINTS FOR FURTHER REFLECTION

1. How can I make sure that my religious beliefs are more than an intellectual exercise but are reflected and actualized in the way I live every day?

2. We all experience actual physical hunger at times, such as when we wake up in the morning. How can I connect this physical feeling with my hunger for God, who alone can satisfy our deepest desires?

3. The divine commands to observe the weekly Sabbath and to embrace fasting as well as feasting as a rhythm of living should help us to be more in control of what we do. How can I use these commands to guard against addiction to work and self-indulgence?

CHAPTER 2:

A Body Humble *Before* God: How *Fasting* Helps Heal Our Relationship *with* God

When you are fasting, do not put on a gloomy look as the hypocrites do: they go about looking unsightly to let people know they are fasting. In truth I tell you, they have had their reward. But when you fast, put scent on your head and wash your face, so that no one will know you are fasting except your Father who sees all that is done in secret; and your Father who sees all that is done in secret will reward you. (Mt 6:16–18)

It is significant that Christian fasting, if it is authentic, has nothing of the grimness and extreme efforts of willpower and self-control. Lent in the Catholic liturgy is called "this joyful season," and in the Orthodox liturgy it is referred to as a time of "bright sadness." Why such paradox? A penitential season can be joyful and bright because it is done communally, a group effort of mutual support and encouragement, and, more importantly, because it redirects our attention away from ourselves and toward God. Grim determination and feats of willpower will get you only so far and are often self-defeating. In the end we come to realize it is only God who saves, and that is such a relief.

Jesus' instructions on fasting are situated within the Gospel According to St. Matthew in the Sermon on the Mount (Mt 5–7). The whole Christian life in all its loftiness and rewards may be found there. The sermon famously begins with the eight beatitudes, the blessings promised to the poor, the sorrowful, the meek, the hungry, the merciful, the pure of heart, the peacemakers, and the persecuted. Jesus then sets forth a higher standard of human behavior, forbidding not just the act of murder but the angry thoughts from which murder arises, not only adultery but adulterous intentions. He requires nonresistance to evildoers and the love of enemies. He teaches the Our Father.

This perfect prayer, the Lord's own, contains among its seven petitions, "Give us this day our daily bread." Jesus thus directs us toward God for our daily sustenance. Notice the significant redundancy in the petition: give us *today* the bread we need for *today*. In this way the Lord anticipates what he will later say in his sermon, "So do not worry about tomorrow: tomorrow will take care of itself. Each day has enough trouble of its own" (Mt 6:34). Note also that another meaning of the Greek word we translate as "daily" is "supersubstantial," something beyond material bread. This is in keeping with the words Jesus used to reject Satan's temptation to turn stones into bread to satisfy his physical hunger: "Human beings live not on bread alone but on every word that comes from the mouth of God" (Mt 4:4).

The Sermon on the Mount as a summary of Christian living makes necessary reference to the three pillars of Jewish piety in the Old Testament—almsgiving, prayer, and fasting. In each of these Jesus places emphasis upon their ultimate purpose, which is not mere exterior practice but rather a recognition of the nature of our relationship with God. We love others, we fast, and we pray in order to fulfill the Great Commandment: "You must love the Lord your God with all your heart, with all your soul, and with all your mind. This is the greatest and the first commandment. The second resembles it: You must love your neighbor as yourself" (Mt 22:37–39).

It has been rightly observed that the shadow of Jesus' own life is all over the Sermon on the Mount.[1] In the beatitudes in particular we find a true portrait of Jesus himself. In the manner also in which Jesus portrays the three pillars of piety, we find the model of how Jesus himself loved others, prayed, and fasted. All three are directed specifically to God. Jesus emphasizes that these things must be done not as acts of self-exhibition but to be seen only by God. The meaning of fasting emerges clearly as an act of humility before God, as a sign of repentance for our sins, and as necessarily accompanied by prayer. Charity toward others is regarded as a true sign that our fasting and prayer have led to a heart truly transformed.

Fasting in the Old Testament

In Mark's gospel, Jesus declares his intent to restore marriage to what it was "at the beginning," referencing the Book of Genesis (Mk 10:6). Genesis is key also in understanding the Old Testament's understanding of fasting. Keep in mind that the "original sin" had to do with eating and, even more significantly, that original sin is the greatest instance of the misuse of the previous gift of human freedom. By directly countering our cravings, fasting helps to restore the original freedom of the children of God and helps us adopt the proper posture before God of humility and vulnerability.

In considering the practice of fasting in the Old Testament, the Book of Joel is a good place to begin. Joel is a prophet, and like all true prophets he speaks for God in unveiling hypocrisy and recalling us to the essential meaning of our religious practices. In Joel's time the Israelites were suffering greatly from a plague of locusts and from drought. Joel interpreted these as signs of God's displeasure. "Order a fast, proclaim a solemn assembly," Joel commands (Jl 1:14). The public fast is to be a sign of interior conversion, he explains:

> But now—declares Yahweh—come back to me with all your heart, fasting, weeping, mourning. Tear your hearts and not your clothes, and come back to Yahweh your God, for he is gracious and compassionate, slow to anger, rich in faithful love (Jl 2:12–13).

The reluctant prophet Jonah, preaching on divine orders to the people of Nineveh, warned, "Only forty days more and Nineveh will be overthrown." To Jonah's disappointment, his non-Jewish audience "believed in God; they proclaimed a fast and put on sackcloth, from the greatest to the least.

When the news reached the king of Nineveh, he rose from his throne, took off his robe, put on sackcloth and sat down in ashes." The king then proclaimed:

> No person or animal, herd or flock, may eat anything; they may not graze, they may not drink any water. All must put on sackcloth and call on God with all their might; and let everyone renounce his evil ways and violent behavior. Who knows? Perhaps God will change his mind and relent and renounce his burning wrath, so that we shall not perish.

The passage concludes, "God saw their efforts to renounce their evil ways. And God relented about the disaster which he had threatened to bring on them, and did not bring it" (Jon 3:4–10).

Both of these prophetic texts, Joel and Jonah, tell us something about fasting and its place in our relationship to God. The text from Joel is read in the liturgy for Ash Wednesday and sets the tone for the whole season. The Church rejoices that the Lord always responds out of love toward his people. Likewise, as the book Jonah teaches us, God awaits our return to him with great mercy.

Another Old Testament book, the Book of the Prophet Isaiah, points to the deeper meaning that must accompany fasting. According to Isaiah, God rejects fasting when it is not accompanied by a true change in how we live.

> Look, you seek your own pleasure on your fastdays, and you exploit all your workmen; look, the only purpose of your fasting is to quarrel and squabble and strike viciously with your fist. Fasting like yours today will never make your voice heard on high. Is that the sort of fast that pleases me, a day when a person inflicts pain on himself? . . .

Is not this the sort of fast that pleases me: to break unjust fetters, to undo the thongs of the yoke. . . . Is it not sharing your food with the hungry, and sheltering the homeless poor; if you see someone lacking clothes, to clothe him, and not to turn away from your own kin? Then your light will blaze out like the dawn and your wound be quickly healed over. Saving justice will go ahead of you and Yahweh's glory come behind you. Then you will cry for help and Yahweh will answer; you will call and he will say, "I am here." (Is 58:3–5, 6–9)

The Book of Judith is enlightening on how fasting should be prayer's partner, an expression in bodily form of what we intend by our words—humble supplication before God who alone brings us salvation.

All the men of Israel cried most fervently to God and humbled themselves before him. They, their wives, their children, their cattle, all their resident aliens, hired or slave, wrapped sackcloth round their loins. All the Israelites in Jerusalem, including women and children, lay prostrate in front of the Temple, and with ashes on their heads stretched out their hands before the Lord. They draped the altar itself in sackcloth and fervently joined together in begging the God of Israel not to let their children be carried off, their wives distributed as booty, the towns of their heritage destroyed, the Temple profaned and desecrated for the heathen to gloat over. The Lord heard them and looked kindly on their distress. The people fasted for many days throughout Judaea as well as in Jerusalem before the sanctuary of the Lord Almighty. (Jdt 4:9–13)

What is impressive about this passage and several of the other ones cited is how fasting was considered a communal practice. Not only adults but children, foreigners, and even domestic animals were expected to join in. Women such as

Judith, Esther, Sarah, and the mothers of Samuel and Samson were models of fasting as a chosen form of piety in which all the people participated. We must also recall that two central moments of the Old Testament—the separate encounters of Moses and Elijah with God upon Mount Sinai—were each preceded by a period of fasting for forty days and nights (Ex 34:28; 1 Kgs 19:8). Among the Jewish people, fasting became a natural manifestation of turning toward God in times of sadness and loss as well as of the need for purification and atonement.

Abraham's Experience of Fasting on Yom Kippur

The Abraham I now speak about is not Abraham of the Bible, the father of many nations and our father in faith, but a young acquaintance of mine who grew up in Brooklyn, New York, in a strict Orthodox Jewish household. Now a devout Catholic, he and his wife each year invite me to their home along with other friends to celebrate Passover.

On one occasion Abraham described how the annual fast on Yom Kippur, the Day of Atonement, was one of the greatest shaping religious experiences of his life. The Torah requires that on the tenth day of the month of Tishri a fast shall be observed for twenty-five hours, beginning at sunset the previous evening and ending at nightfall of the day itself (Lv 23:26ff). On this day each year, God opens the books containing the lives of all persons. He determines who shall live and who shall die during the coming year. Every life is in the balance and all must examine themselves about their transgressions. They must separate themselves from their sins of the past and make a return to the Lord. In ancient times the high priest on this day literally sent a scapegoat into the desert which symbolically carried away the sins of the people.

As Abraham still recalls it, he spent the entire day in the temple crowded with many others. All were fasting from all food, and all were praying. They listened to the admonitions of the scriptures and the rabbi's warnings. "Don't mess with God, Abraham," the rabbi told him. "Do not put any obstacles in his path. Let God do with you what he wills." To this day, one of the deepest impressions that Abraham recalls — besides the feeling of complete vulnerability and abasement before God — was the awareness of a group of people praying and fasting together and the feeling of deep solidarity it created. Before heading home at the end of the services for his first serious meal, he shared food right in the temple where everyone broke their fast together.

Fasting in the New Testament

In the gospels according to Matthew and Luke, Jesus fasted forty days and nights after he was baptized and before beginning his ministry (Mt 4:1–11; Lk 4: 1–13). Jesus' withdrawal into the desert to fast had its precedent in the examples of Moses and Elijah. The forty-day fast also recalls the forty-year testing of the Jewish people in the desert before they reached the land of promise. The period of forty years has a deep meaning here, as forty years was the average lifespan in those times. The Hebrews who had come from Egypt had been slaves there, and still adhered to a slavish mentality. They complained to Moses and Aaron, longing to go back to the way of life they had before:

Why did we not die at Yahweh's hand in Egypt, where we used to sit round the flesh pots and could eat to our heart's content! As it is, you have led us into this desert to starve this entire assembly to death! (Ex 16:3).

All the Hebrews of that generation had to die before the next generation—reared in freedom—could enter the Promised Land. Fasting is about freedom, not slavery. Fasting makes us capable of entering the Promised Land, helping us shed our slavish natures.

As it was for the Israelites, the desert is a place where Jesus faces the temptations of the devil. The three temptations Jesus faces in the desert are these: to turn stones into bread to sustain life; to take unnecessary risks with his life, equivalently putting into question God's providential care; and to divide his heart between the service of God and the pursuit of power and wealth. All three temptations Jesus undergoes relate to the supreme commandment given in the Book of Deuteronomy.

Listen, Israel, Yahweh our God is the one, the only Yahweh. You must love the Yahweh your God with all your heart, with all your soul, with all your strength. (Dt 6:4–5)

What the commandment requires therefore is that we engage and humbly submit nothing less than our deepest self where our very being and desires lie (our heart), our life itself (our soul), as well as all we own and possess (our strength). Jesus responds to all three temptations of the devil by citing passages from Deuteronomy: "Human beings live not on bread alone but on every word that comes from the mouth of Yahweh" (Dt 8:3); "Do not put Yahweh your God to the test" (Dt 6:16); "Yahweh your God is the one you must fear, him alone must you serve" (Dt 6:13).

The temptations Jesus faced in the desert are not peculiar to himself; all of us are tempted at times to live a life of self-indulgence, focusing on our own needs, or to question God's care for us, or to pursue material gain rather than serving God. When the devil suggests that the fasting Jesus satisfy his hunger by turning stones into bread, Jesus points to what he calls his true food and drink which Satan knows nothing of: "My food is to do the will of the one who sent me" (Jn 4:34). By fasting Jesus gives us an example of how to discover beyond ordinary food what will satisfy our deepest longings and desires.

Jesus' response to these three temptations, moreover, shows the clarity of thinking that fasting has provided him, and thus demonstrates the deepest meaning of fasting. Fasting can have a penitential significance, undoing the effects of sin in our lives, but fasting also brings to consciousness our "helplessness, contingency and humbling of self before the omnipotent God who generously guides and sustains life."[2] It was after his fast in the desert that Jesus embarked upon his public ministry, inviting his first disciples. His experience in the desert clarified his thinking, making his path clear. Fasting can do the same for us. It clarifies for us the true path upon which God intends us to walk, in humbleness before our God.

Jesus in his lifetime forbade his disciples to fast (Mt 9:14–17). Fasting, he explained, is meant to show our sorrow at God's absence. Jesus, the divine bridegroom, invites his disciples to rejoice in his presence while he is still with them by feasting, not fasting. In this way Jesus pointed out that fasting is not an end in itself but must always be in reference to God.

St. Paul in the Letter to the Romans gives prominence to the relationship between fasting and charity. Sometimes, he says, we need to give up certain things, even if they are legitimate, for the sake of practicing charity toward others. This teaching of Paul was prompted by the scandal some Christians caused by eating non-kosher foods. Although Paul, following Jesus, acknowledged that such foods were licit, he urged his listeners to eat kosher as an act of personal charity so as not to upset those who continued to observe kosher laws: "For it is not eating and drinking that make the kingdom of God, but the saving justice, the peace and the joy brought by the Holy Spirit" (Rom 14:17).

As the Acts of the Apostles make clear, the early Christians made fasting an integral part of their daily discipleship. For example, when the community had to make decisions, such as the designation of individuals to perform an important ministry, fasting by all was required to discern the Holy Spirit's intentions (Acts 13:2). Once these leaders were chosen, the community gave them their support through prayer and fasting on their behalf (Acts 14:28).

As I was writing this book, a Pentecostal Christian shared with me how fasting was practiced in his household as he was growing up. His father, he said, fasted for a day or more when trying to make up his mind about important matters. He also fasted on behalf of family members who were undergoing a particular crisis. Their church also proclaimed a fast when a member was struggling to overcome an addiction such as smoking. Fasting was seen by all as a response to Paul's command to "be sad with those in sorrow" (Rom 12:15).

A Contemporary Application

One day in a village in Maine, I witnessed a communal event that brought to mind the biblical setting of fasting. Through the village square a long line of people were walking, singly and in groups, all wearing T-shirts that proclaimed the cause for which they were walking. Each had solicited sponsors who made donations to the cause. Boy scouts and girl scouts, members of the high school football team, cheerleaders, members of churches and service organizations, men and women, children and pets were all walking for a common cause. They were happy and proud. They were doing something that engaged their bodies for a spiritual purpose. It was a modern equivalent in a way of the phenomenon described in the Book of Judith. Watching this happening I knew I was seeing a demonstration of the power of communal action in people's lives. In the same way, communal fasting can create a sense of coming together for a greater purpose.

According to a modern dictionary of spirituality and asceticism, a false "spiritualism" has invaded our religious life, one that has precipitated the decline in fasting. We have forgotten, it claims, the need to bring the body into play so as to engage our deepest self in our piety. It concludes:

> The rediscovery of fasting would certainly be an important factor in spiritual renewal. The place fasting once held in the tradition of the Church, its strict connection with biblical anthropology and patristic theology . . . demonstrates that

its engagement is important. The difficulty we have in renewing it derives less from bringing these practices back than from acquiring the rationale for doing them at all. Fasting is a reality that engages body and soul and above all the whole heart where mere ideas cannot work their illusions.[3]

POINTS FOR FURTHER REFLECTION

1. Jesus specifically forbids grimness when we fast. He wants us to appear light-hearted even as we deny ourselves. When I deny myself something, what is my attitude?

2. The true meaning of "conversion" is "turning away." Are there things that my faith has helped me to turn away from? Are there things that I have turned toward as a result?

3. Most of us have some experience of being part of a group, such as a team, in which everyone has acted together. Is my experience of the pillars of Christianity—prayer, fasting, and charity—similar to this, or different?

CHAPTER 3:

A Body Fit *for* Resurrection: What *the* Ancient Ascetics Have *to* Teach Us

Early Christian Practice

In AD 185, in the cosmopolitan city of Alexandria, was born a person who later became known as "the man of steel." His name was Origen, and his writings and example laid the groundwork for the monastic movement which gave birth to Christian asceticism in all its later forms. The son of a Christian martyr, Origen would die in 254 partly because of the suffering he endured in his body for being a Christian. Origen developed a profound knowledge and love of the scriptures which he pondered constantly for the spiritual meanings they contained. He prayed the scriptures into his life, and it is from him that Christians learned *lectio divina* (divine reading) as a method of prayer. It is believed that Anthony of the Desert (250–356), "the first monk," was inspired by his knowledge of Origen's writings. Anthony's life in the desert as popularized by St. Athanasius (297–373) would be the basis for monasticism from then on.

Origen, the Man of Steel

A key to understanding Origen and his influence is the saying that he lived like a Christian and thought like a Greek. Origen, it is said, was always reading, and what he was always reading besides the scriptures themselves was Plato.[1] Origen's Platonic understanding of the distinctive Christian doctrines of the creation, incarnation, and resurrection shaped Christian asceticism but proved problematical.

Following Plato, Origen's thought labored under the weight of an excessive dualism, almost a complete rupture between soul and body. What follows is a significant passage from Plato's *Phaedo*. Here Socrates is portrayed on the day he died proving the immortality of the soul.

> As long as we have our body, and the soul is confused with this evil, we shall never satisfactorily attain the object of our desires, which we say is truth. For the body keeps us busy in a thousand ways through its need of food. Further, disease may hinder us in the pursuit of truth. The body fills us with desires, passions and fears, all kinds of imaginings and nonsense, so that we can never understand by means of it anything in truth and in reality, as we call it. It is the body and its passions that make for wars, revolutions and battles. For all wars are due to the acquisition of wealth, and wealth must be acquired

because of the body, enslaved as we are to its care. And because of all this we have no time for philosophy. Worst of all, when we have some respite from it and proceed to some investigation, it interferes once more at every point in our search, interrupts, disturbs and intimidates us, so that we cannot, because of it, contemplate the truth. We have in fact proved that, if we are ever to have pure knowledge, we must escape from the body and consider things in themselves with our soul [mind] alone. Then, it would seem, we shall realize the wisdom that we desire and love, after death, as our argument shows, not during life.[2]

The Book of Genesis preserves two creation accounts from different sources that are significantly different. With Plato in mind, Origen believed these two accounts are about two different creations, not one. Souls were created first and uniquely bore the divine image and likeness. But the soul's love of God its Creator "cooled," according to Origen, and the soul fell into a body, disrupting the soul's primordial unity with its Creator.

Therefore the path to salvation, thus conceived, was to induce in the soul a state of freedom from all passion through hard asceticism. Origen's message can be distilled in two words: "Be transformed!" Fasting plays a key role in this transformation. Christian ascetics following Origen believed it helped prepare our fallen bodies for their glorious transformation in the resurrection. And the Fall had everything to do with food. Peter Brown explains.

It was widely believed in Egypt and elsewhere that the first sin of Adam and Eve had not been a sexual act but rather ravenous greed. It was their lust for physical food that had led them to disobey God's command not to eat of the fruit of the tree of knowledge. By so doing they had destroyed the perfect equilibrium with which they had been first created. No longer content to contemplate the majesty of God largely (if not wholly) unconscious of the needs of their body, Adam and Eve had reached out to devour the forbidden fruit. In this view of the Fall, greed and in a famine-ridden world, greed's blatant social overtones — avarice and dominance — quite overshadowed sexuality.

To fast for Lent was to undo a little of the fateful sin of Adam. To fast heroically, by living in the desert, the land without food, was to relive Adam's first and most fatal temptation, and to overcome it, as Adam had not done.[3]

In Origen's thinking, the soul, in its fallen state after Adam's sin, was placed by God as a punishment in the temporary material form of the body. According to Peter Brown, the body, for Origen, "was always a limit and a source of frustration. But it was also a frontier that demanded to be crossed."[4] Origen responded to Paul's image of the body as a tent rather than a house. A tent can be folded up at any time as we move to ever more distant frontiers in our spiritual desert crossing. Living in houses, by contrast, was never a feature of the nomadic life of the Jewish people. "The present body," then, according to Origen, "reflected the needs of a single somewhat cramped moment in the spirit's progress back to a former limitless identity."[5]

Much of the thinking of the early Church fathers is along these lines: two modes of human existence, the biological and the personal, and these two are not expressions of but barriers to each other. In this view, the biological realm of primitive instinct deprives us of our freedom and masks the person from others. The Orthodox theologian John

Zizioulas summarizes the appraisal by the early monks regarding the body as

> the tragic instrument which lends to communion with others—stretching out a hand, creating language and speech, conversation, art, kissing. But at the same time it is the mask of hypocrisy, the fortress of individualism, the vehicle of the final separation, death. . . . The tragedy of the biological constitution of man's hypothesis does not lie in his not being a person because of it; it lies in his tending towards becoming a person through it and failing.[6]

Anthony of the Desert, the First Monk

One day a young man, wealthy by the standards of his day, attended Sunday Mass in which the gospel read happened to be the story of Jesus and the rich young man. In the story, Jesus told the man, "If you wish to be perfect, go and sell your possessions and give the money to the poor, and you will have treasure in heaven; then come, follow me" (Mt 19:21). The name of the young man attending Mass that Sunday was Anthony. As it happened, Anthony had recently lost both his parents, leaving his sister and the family farm in his care. Anthony considered himself personally addressed by Jesus. Unlike the rich young man of the gospel, after making provision for his sister, Anthony sold his assets and set out on a path that would lead him from his village on the Nile River to the great desert where he would live for the rest of his life. But not at once.

First, Anthony decided he needed to join what we would call today a fitness club. Before there were any monasteries there were, on the fringes of many villages, small hermitages where committed Christians practiced asceticism by abstaining from sexual relations with their married partner, by fasting, and by extended prayer. Anthony apprenticed himself to one of these ascetics to prepare himself for the rigors of the desert. Anthony spent his days doing manual labor and his nights in prayer. He ate but one meal a day to sustain his strength, and it consisted of bread, salt, and water.

During this valuable time Anthony engaged in what he called "weighing of thoughts." By this he meant the opportunity to conjure up and confront memories from the past and the desires and temptations of the present. Unless he conquered them, he could not endure the life of a solitary in the forbidding desert. Finally, at the age of thirty, Anthony felt ready. But why go to the desert?

Many people think of the desert as a desolate, lifeless place where people can become lost and wander aimlessly. For Anthony the desert was a place where he could practice withdrawal from this world, to see it and himself more clearly. The desert then became for him a place of healing, not only for himself but for the many others who came to him over the years. Anthony gained the reputation of being a healer of souls and bodies. Many sought his wise counsel and became his disciples.

Among such persons was Athanasius, the exiled bishop of Alexandria. Anthony befriended Athanasius during the seventeen long years of his exile, and when Anthony died Athanasius was given the honor of receiving one of the two sheepskins Anthony left as his inheritance. Athanasius was the one who rescued Anthony's life from its obscurity. His widely popular biography, written of the saint in 357, spread the idea of monasticism throughout the Christian world.

Although others before him had lived a similar life of austerity, Anthony became known as the first monk. In the biography Athanasius reports that when potential disciples went out to meet Anthony, they were amazed by his appearance. His body was unchanged even after years of fasting and battling with demons.

Evagrius, Master of the Spiritual Life

Evagrius (345–399) is important in our story of Christian asceticism because he took the insights of Origen and the stunning example of Anthony of the Desert and developed from them a theory of the monastic life that would pass into the ages. In his early life Evagrius was associated with the renowned fathers of the Eastern Church, Basil of Caesarea and Gregory Nazianzus. But it was in the desert and among the monks of Egypt that he learned to decipher "this new alphabet of the heart."[7]

In his book, called in English *The Practice*, Evagrius explains that the spiritual life has as its beginning the development of virtue, the good habits we need for successful living. The cultivation of virtue requires that we strive to eliminate what he called the "evil thoughts," which later became known as the seven deadly sins, namely, gluttony, lust, covetousness, anger, sloth, envy, and pride. Notice that in his listing gluttony leads the rest. It was his belief that food fuels the passions of the body. Since one of the goals of the spiritual life according to Origen is the achievement of "passionlessness," fasting and extended prayer are the only remedies. But Evagrius was wise enough to know that the "deadly thoughts" can never be permanently banished from the human heart. The monk never finishes with asceticism in his entire life.[8]

The monk Cassian (360–435) provided the link to bring these ideas to the West. In his own "institutes" of the monastic life, Cassian describes the second phase of the spiritual journey in terms he learned from Evagrius:

> For we shall never be able to spurn the pleasures of eating here and now if our mind be not fixed on divine contemplation and if it does not take delight, instead, in the love of virtue and the beauty of heavenly things.[9]

The conquering of vice and the cultivation of virtue allow us to contemplate God in all of creation and to enter into communion with him. The heart then becomes free and is given at last the grace of charity, the ultimate goal of our spiritual striving.

Years later, in 553, Origen, Evagrius, and others were condemned by name by the Second Council of Constantinople. Many felt that their Platonist conception of the Christian life created too many problems. But this act, long after their deaths, did not prevent them from having a shaping influence on how we still think of the progress of the soul. The astonishing insight that these thinkers have given us is that "the body can be seen as the 'text' of the soul, the medium for reading the inner workings of the human person."[10] Thus we have a true understanding of the meaning of fasting and how fasting differs from the modern conception of dieting. Dieting focuses only on the body, but fasting focuses on the heart and its transformation. As Peter Brown rightly observes,

> In the desert tradition, the body was allowed to become the discreet mentor of the proud soul. Of all the lessons of

the desert to a late antique thinker, what was most truly astonishing was that the immortal spirit can be purified and refined by clay.[11]

Brown continues:

> It was to the heart and to the strange resilience of the private will that the great tradition of spiritual guidance associated with the Desert Fathers directed its most searching attention. In Adam's first state, the "natural" desires of the heart had been directed toward God, with bounding love and open-hearted awe, in the huge delight of Paradise. It was by reason of Adam's willfulness that these desires had become twisted into a "counter-nature." . . . The great sign of Anthony's recovery of the state of Adam was not his taut body. In his very last year, this state was revealed even more frequently in the quintessential gift of sociability. He came to radiate such magnetic charm and openness to all that any stranger who came upon him, surrounded by crowds of disciples, visiting monks and lay pilgrims, would know him at once, in that dense press of black-garbed figures, which one was the great Anthony. He was instantly recognizable as someone whose heart had achieved total transparency to others.[12]

It is for this reason that hospitality to guests and strangers out of divine charity was the supreme obligation of the monk. Unlike modern dieters, fasting monks would feel compelled to share a meal with any visitor. One ascetic even boasted to having done so several times in the same day.

POINTS FOR FURTHER REFLECTION

1. The goal of early monasticism was the achievement of a passionless existence. How was this ideal both praiseworthy and problematical?

2. What would a spiritual fitness club such as the early hermitages look like today?

3. In what ways is the human body a true text for reading our souls?

CHAPTER 4:

A Body Beautifully Made: The Christian Notion *of the* Person *and* Fasting

Whoever drinks this water will be thirsty again; but no one who drinks the water that I shall give will ever be thirsty again: the water that I shall give will become a spring of water within, welling up for eternal life. (Jn 4:13-14)

The Gospel According to John gives us four definitions by which we may approach the mystery who is God: God is light, God is life, God is truth, and God is love. Light or life or truth or love is not God, for there is no God but God. God, rather, is all of these things in his innermost being, and simultaneously God is the source of these things in all his creatures. God, for example, is both life itself and life-giving.

In my study of St. John's gospel and the other Johannine writings of the New Testament, I was fortunate to have as my professor Donatien Mollat, S.J., who translated these texts and wrote the notes for the Jerusalem Bible. I recall how animated he was as he lectured to us in Latin. When he came to the text that begins this chapter, he was especially excited. The spring of living water that "wells up" into eternal life, he said, in the original Greek refers to the leaping of a living being; as he told us this, he was practically leaping out of his professorial chair at the Gregorian University. Living water is opposed to stagnant water—it is water that flows. It is water that gives life to everything it touches.

Jesus summarized his mission as giving life: "I have come so that they may have life and have it to the full" (Jn 10:10). St. Irenaeus in a memorable phrase said that "the glory of God is the human person who is fully alive." Another of the early Church fathers, Origen, said that "God takes away all deadness in us." Deadness can invade our lives, but fasting can be a remedy to help us restore good physical and spiritual health.

A Body Beautifully Made

> God said, "Let us make man in our own image, in the likeness of ourselves." (Gn 1:26)

In this chapter we dispel any notion of self-hatred or self-punishment as a motive for fasting. On the contrary we will affirm the fundamental goodness of the human person in all aspects of his or her life, including the physical. We will explain the uniqueness of the human person amidst all the others of God's creatures, our social nature, and the precious gift of freedom. We first look to the Book of Genesis and to Christ himself, who cited it in order to explain how things were "at the beginning" (Mt 19:4). We will go on, in our exposition of Genesis, to see how all of these qualities were affected by the misuse of our freedom in an event that became known as "the Fall." Finally, we will see how fasting is a necessary tool in our restoration and in the healing of our existence, which even today is burdened by this "original sin." In our present disorder, fasting is a way "to keep body and soul together."

Genesis

"O God, help me to believe the truth about myself, no matter how beautiful it is!" This anonymous prayer is a magnificent distillation of the teaching of the Book of Genesis about human nature as coming from God's creative hand. A sense of awe and wonder pervades the two accounts of creation in the Bible. Again and again, in the first story, God pauses after God makes each creature to declare how good it is. The human person is made last in the first account and first in the second, but the intention is the same — to highlight human uniqueness. Only when the human person is made does God pronounce it is not only good but "very good" (Gn 1:31).

"Goodness" in this case does not mean something merely useful or practical, but rather "beautiful." The process of creation is not like a mechanical making but more like an artistic production in which the artist of necessity endows his work of art with stylistic traces of himself. St. Augustine in his *Confessions* expresses his appreciation of God's creation in these very terms.

> You, therefore, O God, who are beautiful, made these things, for they are beautiful; you who are good made them, for they are good; you who are made them, for they are. Yet they are not so good, nor are they so beautiful as you, nor do they even be in such wise as you, their creator. Compared to you, they are neither good nor beautiful nor real.[1]

The psalms of the Bible are filled with admiration for God's creative powers as expressed in the universe and especially in the incredible God-like being who is the human person.

> Yahweh our Lord,
> how majestic is your name throughout the world! . . .
> I look up at your heavens, shaped by your fingers,
> at the moon and the stars you set firm —
> what are human beings that you spare a thought for them,
> the child of Adam that you can care for him?

> Yet you have made him little less than a god,
> you have crowned him with glory and beauty,
> made him lord of the works of your hands,
> put all things under his feet. (Ps 8:1, 3–6)

It is truly astonishing that in a monotheistic religion like that of the Bible, in which God is completely unique and spiritual, a creature, the human, is said to have been made in God's own image and likeness. God, according to Genesis, entrusts everything God has made to his human representative for its care and good order. To the human alone is given the authority to give the other creatures their names (Gn 2:20).

Another indication of human dignity is the observance of the Sabbath rest (Gn 2:2). Other religions had annual or semi-annual festivals, but the Jewish religion had a weekly festival in which humans were enjoined to rest from their labors and contemplate the glory of God and of creation. In this conception the human person is no mere beast of burden whose worth is to be defined by what he produces. According to Genesis, we are to work in order to live, not live in order to work.

The second creation story in Genesis conveys two other essential human qualities: our fundamentally social nature and the amazing gift of personal freedom. "It is not right that the man should be alone," God declares, "I shall make him a helper" (Gn 2:18). The "helper," woman, is fashioned from a rib taken from the first man to indicate that each shares the same human nature and dignity. God then directs the man and the woman in their idyllic life in the garden of Eden not to eat of the fruit of the tree of the knowledge of good and evil — but they do (Gn 2:3). Humans thus used their gift of freedom to say no to God their creator, and the consequences are disastrous.

They now hide themselves from God and engage in mutual recrimination. They become ashamed of their physicality and cover their nakedness. Human labor becomes arduous rather than joyful. They are expelled from the garden and death enters the world for the first time, not just death by so-called "natural" causes but fratricide. God's question, "What have you done?" (Gn 4:10), echoes down the ages. In one of the saddest of all the sad verses of the Bible, we learn "Yahweh regretted having made human beings on earth and was grieved at heart" (Gn 6:6).

It is against this background and profound understanding of the human condition in both its glory and degradation that we must approach the concept of fasting.

St. Augustine and Our Unruly Desires

One of the main consequences of original sin, the fallen human condition into which each of us has been born, is what St. Augustine of Hippo (354–430) termed "concupiscence," or disordered desires. St. Augustine made this discovery by looking within his own heart, and being dismayed and frustrated about what he found there. He has been called the "doctor of grace" because he came to understand that only God's grace, not his own unaided efforts, could rid him of this terrible burden. As he tells us in his autobiography, *The Confessions*, he found his heart perpetually unstable, always tumbling off balance toward what it wants, not knowing what it might be.

In *The Confessions* Augustine looks back to his adolescence and describes a troubling incident. To us it might seem trivial, but to him it revealed the whole psychology of his unruly passions. He and a group of friends came upon a pear tree on his neighbor's property. In a random and thoughtless act, they decided to shake the tree and steal its fruit—for no reason. He explains:

> I stole a thing of which I had plenty of my own and of much better quality. Nor did I wish to enjoy the thing which I desired to gain by theft, but rather to enjoy the actual theft and the sin of theft. . . . Foul was the evil and I loved it.[2]

This thoughtless, anxious grasping for something, for anything, is what St. Augustine diagnoses as "concupiscence." It is a state of being out of control. It means regularly choosing, to our dismay, something inferior even when we know it is inferior. Referring to a passage from the letters of St. Paul, Augustine says, "Thus I understood from my own experience what I had read, how 'the flesh lusts against the spirit and the spirit against the flesh' (Gal 5:17). I was in both camps."[3] It is important to note that the "flesh" here does not refer to the body but to the prideful selfishness, with all its deadening effects, that can take over and control both our bodies and our souls. St. Peter in his second epistle refers to it as "disordered passion," whose antidote is "self-control" (2 Pt 1:4–6).

Augustine scholar Margaret Miles, in her book *Fullness of Life: Historical Foundations for a New Asceticism*, demonstrates the relevance for us of Augustine's concept of concupiscence and its ultimate healing through God's grace. Her definition of concupiscence is "repetition syndrome," the tendency to do something repeatedly, even when doing it brings us less and less satisfaction. Explaining Augustine's dilemma, she quotes him as saying, "I hesitated to die to deadness and live to life."[4] This "deadness" comes from the inertia and habit of concupiscence. Its cure comes when by God's grace we are enabled to love God above all and to love others in God and not simply as a means to satisfy our own selfishness. "Just as the soul is the whole life of the body," Augustine wrote in his classic work on free will, "so God is the blessed life of the soul."[5] Miles concludes, "The unity of body and soul was a continuing source of wonder, puzzlement and conjecture for [Augustine]. . . . He moved more and more to the opinion that the human body is simply the condition of human learning, trial and ultimate victory."[6]

Karl Rahner, S.J., is noted among modern theologians for his classic essays on the subject of concupiscence and its relevance for us. Following the insights of Augustine and modern transcendental philosophy, Rahner defines concupiscence as the spontaneous desires and appetites that precede our free-will decisions and impede them. They can eventually take over our lives through habits of thinking and acting that come to define us as persons. Like Augustine, Rahner attributes our ultimate healing to God's grace which allows us to cultivate the new virtues, the powers that allow us to become the persons we truly wish to be.[7]

Miles speaks vividly of our culturally endorsed addictions to power, sex, and possession, the very three "temptations" Jesus was able to overcome fasting in the desert. She speaks specifically about "such prevalent practices in our culture as alcoholism, promiscuity, overeating, drug dependence, overwork, an inhuman pace of life and environmental pollution."[8] We need to fast from these to recover health — physical, mental, and spiritual.

Keeping Body and Soul Together

Almost daily in the media we see instances where people, for one reason or another, do what might be called uncharacteristic things — people otherwise well put-together completely losing it. To take just one example, the public was astonished when Lisa Nowak, a Navy captain and astronaut, married mother of three, drove nine hundred and fifty miles to confront another woman she believed was involved with a man other than her husband with whom she had fallen in love. No doubt the stress of traveling into space and back again was a contributing factor, but still people asked themselves, "Why would an intelligent, accomplished person do such a thing?" Then there was a report about a Belgian skydiver who was believed to have sabotaged another diver's parachute and watched her fall thirteen thousand feet to her death. According to the police report, the suspicion was that she did this because the other diver was romantically involved with her boyfriend.

Anthropologists have a name for this: it is termed "wanting-seeking syndrome." It is an intense form of craving that makes people engage in dangerous behavior and experience an unusual level of anger. Anthropologists describe this condition as similar to other extreme behaviors such as road rage. The explanation of road rage is that it's not really about someone driving badly, about someone cutting you off. It is rather the manifestation of an old wound: "They always disrespected me."[9] What scientists call "wanting-seeking syndrome," that "old wound" that keeps on surfacing and makes us do irrational and self-destructive things, is an expression of the disordered human condition, what we have been referring to as "original sin." As we have explained, original sin is not the same as the personal sins we commit on our own, but refers to the condition of the world we inherit and are born into that affects our ability to make decisions.

But how do we protect ourselves from giving in to our disordered human condition? St. Augustine found helpful a passage from St. Paul's letters in which the apostle compares himself to an athlete, a runner or a boxer, who must undergo strenuous physical training to achieve victory. Paul writes:

Do you not realize that, though all the runners in the stadium take part in the race, only one of them gets the prize? Run like that—to win. Every athlete concentrates completely on training, and this is to win a wreath that will wither, whereas ours will never wither. So that is how I run, not without a clear goal; and how I box, not wasting my blows on air. I punish my body and bring it under control, to avoid the risk that, having acted as a herald for others, I myself may be disqualified. (1 Cor 9:24–27)

The rigorous regime of training that Augustine recommends is the traditional one that we have been describing, the practice of the three pillars of piety. He writes:

Therefore the Lord in the Gospels . . . declared in his exposition of righteousness itself that there is none except these three—fasting, alms and prayer. Now in fasting he indicates the entire subjugation of the body; in alms, all kindness of will and deeds, either by giving or forgiving; and in prayers, he implies all the rules of holy desire. Although by the subjugation of the body, a check is given to the concupiscence which ought not only to be bridled but to be put altogether out of existence . . . yet it often excites its immoderate desires even in the use of things which are allowable and right.[10]

From what Augustine says it becomes clear that just paying attention to our physical emotions and needs is not enough. In addition, we must do the important soul work of cultivating new and more sound desires, which we can learn only through our personal conversation with God in prayer and by loving others as Christ loved them, in a love that is self-giving, and for their own sake rather than for our own needs and personal agenda.

The Body for the Glory of God

The words of St. Paul given above, especially what he describes as "punishing the body in order to subdue it," should not be misunderstood as a disparagement of the physical side of our lives. He would add that the proud soul also needs to be subdued in the fight for personal freedom. In the Christian understanding of the human person, the body is in fact the whole person as an embodied reality, and therefore we profess our belief in the resurrection of the body as part of our total and complete salvation. We cannot imagine a future existence for ourselves as human beings apart from our bodies. Thus Paul in the First Letter to the Corinthians makes reference to our becoming—through our participation in Christ's resurrection—"spiritual bodies." Such a body is one that is to be understood as filled and animated with the Spirit of God who becomes our life principle.

In Jewish-Christian anthropology, the human person exists in three dimensions: body, mind, and spirit. The center of the human person, in this view, is something called the "heart." No mere physical organ, the heart is the human person's capacity—or incapacity—to open up to God and others. The prophetic message in the Bible aims directly at the heart. Ezekiel declares, "I shall give you a new heart, and put a new spirit in you; I shall remove the heart of stone from your bodies and give you a heart of flesh instead" (Ez 36:26). Jesus himself, speaking as a prophet, named among the beatitudes "purity of heart." "Blessed are the pure in heart: they shall see God" (Mt 5:8). A pure heart is one that is undivided, not torn between selfishness and devotion to God. Søren Kierkegaard defined purity of heart as "to will one thing."

The total transformation of the human person in baptism is accomplished by giving to mind, heart, and spirit a new life principle: the gift of the Holy Spirit. The same Spirit raised Jesus from the dead "so that the life of Jesus . . . may be visible in our mortal flesh" (2 Cor 4:11). A body reborn by the Spirit's power is not its own anymore but a member of Christ and a temple of the Holy Spirit. Thus, Paul writes, "use your body for the glory of God" (1 Cor 6:20). Commenting on this stunning passage, Jerome Murphy-O'Connor, O.P., states that the body is the sphere in which commitment to Christ becomes real, for, he says, "there is no such thing as a purely spiritual Christianity."[11]

Toward a Theology of the Body

A temple or a tomb. These seem to be the two contrasting estimations of the human body. St. Paul calls the body a temple (1 Cor 6:19), but as we saw in the previous chapter there is much in early Christian history to make you believe, along with Plato, that it is more of a tomb. With the coming of the Middle Ages, a more positive appreciation of the body began to emerge. St. Thomas Aquinas clearly taught that the soul is the "form" of the body, that is, the person is a body and does not merely "have" a body. In her pioneering book on the practice of fasting by women in the middle ages, *Holy Feast and Holy Fast: The Religious Significance of Food to Medieval Women*, Caroline Walker Bynum notes that in the twelfth century the body was becoming more and more central in Christian reflection and piety. Fasting rules, for example, became less stringent so that working laypeople could practice them, not just the religious professionals living in monastic enclosure.

Marriage for the first time was counted among the seven sacraments instituted by Jesus, whereas in earlier times its association with the sexual component of human life made it seem less connected with spiritual realities.

In the Christian faith, the central mysteries of creation, incarnation, and resurrection all have to do with the body. It is Bynum's contention that compared with the range and richness of medieval understandings of the meaning of the body and of food, our present-day understandings of these same things appear more narrow and negative. Our therapies to help those suffering from "eating disorders" often fail because they do not address adequately the beauty of the body and are based more upon exercising greater control over ourselves, which is precisely the problem. Bynum therefore challenges "the standard interpretation of asceticism as world rejection or as a practical dualism, and of the standard picture of medieval women as constrained on every side by a misogyny they internalized as self-hatred and masochism." Rather, she writes, "I argue that medieval efforts to discipline and manipulate the body should be interpreted more as elaborate changes rung upon the *possibilities* provided by fleshiness than as flights from physicality." She concludes,

> Late medieval asceticism was an effort to plumb and to realize all the possibilities of the flesh. It was a profound expression of the doctrine of the incarnation: the doctrine that Christ, by becoming human, saves all that the human being is.[12]

Closer to our own time, shortly after being elected pope, John Paul II set out what he ambitiously called "the theology of the body." He elaborated this theology in a series of talks he gave at his regular weekly public audiences between

September 5, 1979, and April 2, 1980. The pope argues that from the beginning "the human person is in the visible world as a body among bodies and discovers the meaning of his own bodiliness." He continues:

> Man is a subject not only because of his self-awareness and self-determination but also as the basis of his own body. The structure of this body is such as to permit him to be the author of truly human activity. In this activity the body expresses the person. The body, therefore, in all its materiality, is almost penetrable and transparent, in such a way as to make clear who man is.[13]

In a footnote to these passages the pope comments, "The dualistic contraposition of 'soul-body' does not appear in the conception of the most ancient books of the Bible."[14]

Joseph Ratzinger, the present Pope Benedict XVI, in his book on eschatology likewise sees a close connection between body and soul:

> And so we come at last to a really tremendous idea: the human spirit is so utterly one with the body that the term "form" can be used of the body and retain its proper meaning. Conversely, the form of the body is spirit, and this is what makes the body a person. . . . We can truly say then that the body is the soul's visibility. Body and soul are related to one another as expression and being expressed.[15]

Pope Benedict chose his first encyclical, *Deus caritas est* (God is Love), to give particular attention to the body and the erotic component of love, human and divine, construed in a highly positive way. On the other hand, he argues, a one-sided focus on the body can have the opposite effect of separating the body from the person.

The contemporary way of exalting the body is deceptive. *Eros* reduced to pure "sex" has become a commodity, a mere "thing" to be bought and sold, or, rather, man himself becomes a commodity. This is hardly man's great "yes" to the body. On the contrary, he now considers his body and his sexuality as the purely material part of himself, to be used and exploited at will. Nor does he see it as an arena for the exercise of freedom, but as a mere object that he attempts, as he pleases, to make both enjoyable and harmless. Here we are actually dealing with the debasement of the human body: no longer is it integrated into our overall existential freedom; no longer is it a vital expression of our whole being, but it is more or less relegated to the purely biological sphere. The apparent exaltation of the body can quickly turn into a hatred of bodiliness. Christian faith, on the other hand, has always considered man a unity in duality, a reality in which spirit and matter copenetrate and each is brought to a new nobility. True, *eros* tends to rise in ecstasy toward the Divine, to lead us beyond ourselves; yet for this very reason it calls for a path of ascent, renunciation, purification and healing.[16]

Finally, as noted above, of crucial importance in our understanding of the body is the core Christian belief in what the East calls "the resurrection of the body" and the West "the resurrection of the flesh." The soul that survives bodily death still retains its nature as a spirit related to a body. Only as embodied does the human person achieve its perfection. The West refers to the resurrection of the "flesh," a Hebrew concept that places the body within God's creation. Creatures retain a basic relatedness to the Creator and if they are open to it, they can receive the fullness of life from God who is life itself.

POINTS FOR FURTHER REFLECTION

1. There are certain behaviors that St. Augustine labels "concupiscence" and others label "repetition syndrome." What behaviors in my life could be described this way?

2. Our culture often encourages us to minimize our vulnerability and dependence in favor of appearing confident. Do I feel able to express and accept my own vulnerability?

3. A temple or a tomb? What images of the body do we encounter in our daily lives? How can we evaluate these from a Christian perspective?

CHAPTER 5:

A Body Socially Responsible: How Fasting Grounds *Our* Solidarity *with* Others

Instead, I tell you, be guided by the Spirit, and you will no longer yield to self-indulgence. . . . When self-indulgence is at work the results are obvious: sexual vice, impurity, and sensuality, the worship of false gods and sorcery; antagonisms and rivalry, jealousy, bad temper and quarrels, disagreements, factions and malice, drunkenness, orgies and all such things. . . . On the other hand the fruit of the Spirit is love, joy, peace, patience, kindness, goodness, trustfulness, gentleness and self-control. (Gal 5:16, 19–20, 22–23)

You ask us to express our thanks by self-denial. We are to master our sinfulness and conquer our pride. We are to show to those in need your goodness to ourselves. (Lenten Preface III)

Fasting and Social Charity

In our survey of biblical teachings regarding fasting, we noted that the ultimate motive and grounding of fasting is to move the heart toward compassion and social charity. Isaiah, to cite one notable example, portrays God as rejecting our fasting and our prayers unless they are accompanied by "sharing your food with the hungry, and sheltering the homeless poor" (Is 58:7). The Church selects this very passage to inaugurate Lent on Ash Wednesday in the liturgy of the hours.

It was St. Augustine who provided a memorable image of two wings to show how our prayers will only reach God if they are borne aloft by fasting and deeds of charity.

> Break your bread for those who are hungry, said Isaiah, do not believe that fasting suffices. Fasting chastises you, but it does not refresh the other. Your privations shall bear fruit if you give generously to another. . . . Do you wish your prayer to reach God? Give it two wings, fasting and almsgiving.[1]

The early Christians, as we have seen, in their practice of fasting always had social charity in mind. On the days when they were not fasting, the hermits of the desert typically had their one meal of the day at three in the afternoon. The meal consisted of two small loaves of hard bread seasoned with salt and water. Lentils, beans, and fruit were reserved for visitors and for the sick. Wine and meat were never taken. This meal was the basic diet of the poor Egyptian peasant. In this setting it is easy to understand why gluttony was at the very top of the seven "evil thoughts" or capital sins: it was not merely because these ascetics believed that the desire for food and the arousal of the passions were related, but because in lands where famine and starvation were common, eating to excess and desiring to do so were social sins.

A telling passage from the *Didache*, the so-called teaching of the twelve apostles, written in the second century after Christ, makes clear the link between fasting and social charity among the early Christians. Those who had left all to announce the good news were to be greeted as if they were the Lord himself. To support them during their visits to the scattered communities of Christians, and to give alms to the poor, the *Didache* reports that Christian households had to fast for days and days.[2]

The women of the Middle Ages who fasted were not fixated on bodily appearance. As Caroline Walker Bynum explains:

> To stress women's food practices and concerns as control of body is to focus too narrowly on fasting—on not eating. In fact . . . women's fasting was part of a broader pattern of behavior. . . . Women's fasting was explicitly seen, by women themselves and by their confessors and advisers, as preparation both for receiving the Eucharist and for almsgiving. Women gave to the poor and sick the food they denied themselves; women cleansed their bodies of prosaic food in order to ready them for the coming of the food that was Christ.[3]

Social charity is a defining characteristic of Christian fasting. One of the main reasons Christians fast is to fight against innate human selfishness and possessiveness, and to resist the social forces that drive us to consume more and more of the earth's resources at the expense of the poor. They fast to practice solidarity with the poor by practicing the virtue of temperance.

I use the term "social charity" following Pope Benedict XVI, who taught in *Deus caritas est* that charity is constitutive of the preaching of the gospel and of the Church's identity. Individual Christians as citizens, inspired by the gospel, have the duty to engage in the political process to achieve greater justice for all, but the specific service the Church itself is charged to carry out is the service of charity, in the pope's phrasing: "to attend constantly to man's sufferings and his needs, including his material needs."[4]

The time is right for a renewal of the religious practice of fasting specifically motivated by social charity. Ethical eating is very much in the public consciousness. Well-known restaurateurs are refusing to serve meat produced by factory methods, eggs from industrial chickens, and species of fish that are endangered. The emphasis upon locally grown food is another example of the ethical revolt in our eating habits against purely economic concerns. Professor John E. Carroll writes in his book, *The Wisdom of Small Farms and Local Foods:*

> One of our most basic and predominant human activities is to eat. If the supply of food cannot come from the lands around us, land which we see and feel much of the time, then such lands can never be kept available for the feeding of future generations. So health, in body, mind and spirit, is what it's all about. Environmental pollution from fossil fuel uses and other sources in our modern economy, climate change, the geopolitics of foreign oil all contribute

to a rationale in support of local food for local people, but if we don't have health in all three forms, body, mind and spirit, what does the rest matter?[5]

Fasting in Solidarity with the Poor

The federal food stamp program helps feed twenty-six million persons in the United States who do not earn enough to feed themselves. During the deliberations in Congress in 2007 about this program, one representative decided to try to live for just one week on the three dollars a day a typical food stamp recipient is given by the government. His wife joined him in an effort to gain people's attention and raise their awareness about the existence of hunger in this most prosperous nation. During these seven days the representative lost three pounds. The last night before the experiment, the couple dined on steaks, asparagus, tomatoes, and a bottle of pinot noir. The next morning their breakfast consisted of a banana accompanied by water from the tap, but no coffee — coffee was too expensive. Pasta, rice, and frozen vegetables got them through the week. Their conclusion was that no one should be forced to live on such meager rations. America in this regard is far better off than such regions as sub-Saharan Africa where thirty-three million children under five years old are starving and face stunted futures if they survive at all.

Catholic social teaching is based upon the principles of justice, the common good, and solidarity with others, especially the most vulnerable. It requires modifications in how we live our lives, particularly in our eating habits. Solidarity is that form of social charity and friendship with others that forces us to reevaluate how we eat. Self-centered, mindless consumption of the earth's scarce goods in disregard of others' needs may be described as a social sin.

According to Catholic social teaching, private ownership of the goods of the earth, even legitimately acquired, does not cancel what is called their "universal destination." Because the earth ultimately belongs only to God, private ownership is basically restricted in its use to serve the common good. No one has the right to live at the expense of others.[6] To give one example, globalization, in the sense of free and open markets, cannot be allowed to function without constraint if local populations are made to suffer harm; economic and technical progress must serve people, not deprive them of their livelihoods. In this regard I vividly recall a conversation that I had several years ago with an international banker; he revealed that banking institutions such as his own prefer to give loans to poorer nations with unstable political situations because after each coup d'état the banks can renegotiate their loans at rates even more favorable to the banks.

As is increasingly clear, the peace of the world can be assured only if all the peoples in it feel they are benefiting from human progress and are not destined to be a permanent, exploited underclass. The international media make such disparities in living standards apparent to people no matter where they live. As Pope John Paul II taught, there is an "equal right of all people to take their seat at the table of the common banquet."[7]

The practice of the virtue of solidarity frees us from the consumer mentality according to which everything is just a commodity, something to be consumed. A commodity may be described as a good of the earth separated from its original context and its interrelatedness with everything else. Persons used to living their chosen "lifestyle" need to become conscious that their consumer choices manifest their ethics.

A truly frightening, apocalyptic vision of our consumerist future in America may be found in a recent novel aimed at a teenage audience: *Feed*, by M. T. Anderson. It is rightly receiving much comment because of its social relevance. As the novel opens, consumerist America has reached its final days. Rioting has broken out in malls across the country. All of nature has become denuded, mysterious lesions are appearing on the bodies of the population. The moon has become our fifty-first state, but a global alliance is threatening to attack. People are becoming increasingly disoriented by their "feeds," tiny chips inserted at birth into their brains that provide useful consumer information in every life situation. The schools have become the exclusive domain of major corporations, and their purpose is to teach people "how to work technology and how to find bargains and what's the best way to get a job and how to decorate our bedroom."[8] As one of the novel's major characters sums it all up, "We Americans are interested only in the consumption of our products. We have no interest in how they were produced, or what happens to them when we discard them, once we throw them away."[9] This dystopian world, where everything is discardable, including human relationships, is a powerful manifestation of what could happen in the absence of solidarity.

Fasting and the Virtue of Temperance

The Christian virtues of temperance and repentance have long been given as the primary motivations for the practice of fasting. They are the principal remedies for the human tendency toward dissipation and carelessness. At its most basic level, the regular practice of fasting serves as a reminder in our distracted existence to pay attention to what we are eating. But fasting can also be the daily occasion to practice the virtue of temperance.

Temperance, along with prudence, justice, and fortitude, has long been called one of the four "cardinal" or "hinge" virtues that define a person and permit us to live a complete and fulfilling life. To be temperate means far more than being moderate in our habits. Moderation in the sense of "portion control" is only a small part of the virtue of temperance. A person who is temperate lives a life in which all aspects of being are kept in unity and balance, a life that is well-ordered in all ways. According to Josef Pieper in his classic work, *The Four Cardinal Virtues*, "temperance counteracts our natural tendency to self-preservation and to selfishness. It provides the discipline we need to achieve the serenity of a well-ordered existence."[10]

Fasting is one way to become a temperate person. Thus for St. Thomas Aquinas fasting is part of the natural law, not just Christian ethics, because everyone must strive to become a free moral agent in fundamental possession of himself.[11] Temperance by no means is on a par with Christian charity, but temperance in the form of fasting can open the way and provide the possibility for divine charity to transform our hearts.

The Personal Witness of Simone Weil

It may be that vice, depravity and crime are nearly always attempts to eat beauty, to eat what we should only look at. Eve began it. If she caused humanity to be lost by eating the fruit, the opposite attitude, looking at the fruit without eating it, should be what is required to save it.

If I grow thin from labor in the fields, my flesh really becomes wheat. If that wheat is used for the host it becomes Christ's flesh. Anyone who labors with this intention becomes a saint.[12]

Simone Weil died on September 3, 1943, in exile from France in England, at the age of thirty-four, having starved herself to death. Suffering from tuberculosis, she refused, in solidarity with her countrymen in Nazi-occupied France, to eat more than they were able to eat. She stands as a witness to social justice and to the significance and hazards of religious fasting.

According to George Steiner, "there has been in the Western tradition only one woman philosopher of rank: Simone Weil."[13] Her philosophical writings include *Gravity and Grace, Waiting for God*—both of which were assembled from notes she left at her death—and *The Need for Roots*, her masterpiece. Weil also has been revered as a saint, "one of the most remarkable women of our time, one who can be placed with Teresa of Avila and with the two Catherines, of Genoa and Siena."[14] She has also been reviled as the "advocate of a bogus Christianity, a lost cause and a self-hating personal disaster."[15]

No one can question that Weil's philosophical works were not mere academic exercises. They are passionate essays about the mortal dangers of Hitlerism, Stalinism, and

Western colonialism, as well as expositions of the hunger for God and the need for spiritual roots. When Simone Petremont's biography of Weil appeared in English, Elizabeth Hardwick's review went to the heart of the matter:

> The willed deprivation of her last period was not new; indeed refusal seems to have been a part of her character since infancy. What sets her apart from our current ascetics with their practice of transcendental meditation, diet, vegetarianism, ashram simplicities, yoga, is that with them the depravities and rigors are undergone for the pay-off—for tranquility, for thinness, for the hope of a long life—or frequently, it seems, to fill the hole of emptiness so painful to the narcissist. With Simone Weil it was entirely the opposite.
>
> It was her wish, or her need, to undergo misery, affliction and deprivation because such had been the lot of mankind throughout history. Her wish was not to feel better but to honor the sufferings of the lowest.[16]

Weil's contemporary, Simone de Beauvoir, had a similar impression. Beauvoir and Weil took the entrance examinations for admission to the École Normale Supérieure at the same time. Weil came out first, Beauvoir second, as Beauvoir recalled.

> She intrigued me, because of her great reputation for intelligence and her bizarre outfits. . . . A great famine had broken out in China, and I was told that when she heard the news she had wept: these tears compelled my respect much more than her gifts as a philosopher. I envied her for having a heart that could beat right across the world.[17]

For Easter 1938, Weil, the daughter of assimilated Jews who taught their daughter she was French first and foremost, traveled to the Benedictine abbey of Solesmes. It became a religious turning point. The ancient liturgies and chants impressed her deeply, but it was a poem by George Herbert that someone gave her there at the monastery that provided her first revelation of Christ: "The poem helped Weil to experience for the first time the tender goodness of God," according to her biographer.[18]

> "Love"
> Love bade me welcome; yet my soul drew back,
> Guiltie of dust and sin.
> But quick-eyed Love, observing me grow slack
> From my first entrance in,
> Drew nearer to me, sweetly questioning
> If I lack'd anything.
>
> A guest, I answer'd, worthy to be here.
> Love said, You shall be he.
> I, the unkinde, ungrateful? Ah, my deare,
> I cannot look on thee.
> Love took my hand and smiling did reply:
> Who made the eyes but I?
>
> Truth, Lord; but I have marr'd them; let my shame
> Go where it doth deserve.
> And know you not, says Love, who bore the blame?
> My deare, then I will serve.
> You must sit down, says Love, and taste my meat.
> So I did sit and eat.

From that moment Weil never doubted Christ's divinity. From that moment she embraced the vocation of a mystic like "the saints and doctors of the church and the visionaries of the Middle Ages and the Baroque."[19] Hunger for God, the food which only God can supply, was at the heart of Weil's experience of fasting.

The psychologist Robert Coles puzzled, like many others, about why Weil was so hard on herself. Was she suffering from anorexia? Was she crazy? He came to this explanation:

> As for Simone Weil, her hunger was for God, not a slim waist-line. . . . Her intense moral imagination simply couldn't stop doing its work, couldn't stop distracting her from the routines the rest of us take for granted, including our meals. She refused the food offered her while awaiting the big feast she often mentioned, the one given the symbolic form of Holy Communion. She yearned to have her appetite appeased, not for a day or for a week, Sunday to Sunday, but forever."[20]

It is no doubt hard, if not impossible from this distance, to share the experience of Simone Weil, a woman, a Jew, a philosopher, and a mystic in the extreme circumstances of the Second World War. Her surviving essays bear the burnt holes of her ceaseless smoking. "She wrote," it has been observed, "with a sense of desperate urgency, eating next to nothing, and living mainly on wine, coffee and cigarettes."[21] Weil perhaps finds her true context within the early Christian desert mystics who saw through the world and diagnosed its spiritual illness in the light of an overwhelming experience of divine love. The Weil who, despite her frail condition, did rigorous factory work to experience the actual life of such workers; who joined in the Spanish Civil War until an injury forced her to withdraw; who could have remained with her parents in the safety of New York City, but chose to return to Europe during the World War II; who petitioned Charles de Gaulle to be parachuted behind enemy lines to nurse the wounded, but was given instead the "busy-work" that became *The Need for Roots*: this Weil was the one who chose fasting as her expression of solidarity with all who were starving.

Other Personal Examples

In the writing of this book I was in contact with one of my former seminarians at the North American College in Rome who is a Catholic priest of an Eastern rite and a seminary professor. He and the other Byzantine and Maronite seminarians taught me much about the riches of the Eastern liturgical traditions and ascetical practices. In passing he made reference to solidarity with the poor as very much part of the Byzantine tradition of fasting and his own personal practice of it. He admits "this would have been more obvious in other times and places when the poor were subsistent vegetarians." It is not quite as clear "when the urban poor live on whatever the 7-Eleven sells ready-made: corn dogs, cheesy puffs and Mountain Dew super-sized." He continued, "In theory, the Lenten diet (especially eating raw or merely boiled vegetables) should save plenty of time and money. The time should go to prayer and the money should go to charity." He concludes, "Even living alone, cutting out meat, dairy and wine, led to savings of $50 or more a week — $350 for charity during the seven weeks of Lent."[22]

I am much impressed with how enthusiastically youth in this country and around the world have become attracted to the practice of fasting precisely from the motivation of helping the poor. For example, at a Sunday Mass in Singapore that I participated in, I was handed a copy of the archdiocesan newspaper which carried an article about youths aged from fourteen to twenty-three who "stepped into the shoes of the suffering and poor of Asia" by participating in a twenty-four-hour fast. "By literally fasting," the article explained, "these youth experienced hunger and poverty, and were able to reflect on issues of globalization and oppression." The project in which they participated is called FAST—"For Asia Solidarity Together."

The Singapore project actually was inspired by a similar program in Brunei conducted the previous Lent for Catholic youth. It consisted of a thirty-hour fast accompanied by sessions on mission and poverty. One of the Singaporeans commented,

> We were very touched by the eagerness of the youths as young as thirteen years old coming together to fast for a cause. These young people were as affluent as our Singapore youths and they were willing to give up all comforts and food for thirty hours. There was great solidarity and energy. One would not have guessed that thirty hours later, the youths had not taken a single bite, not even a drop of milk. They were still energetic, vibrant and praising God.[23]

For some years now I have been recommending what is called the "Skip a Meal" program as a simple way to introduce greater fasting in our daily life, especially during the Lenten season. I like it because it combines in a single practice fasting, prayer, and social charity. It was introduced to me by a group of Buddhist laypeople with whom I attended a conference in Italy of the World Conference on Religion and Peace. It goes like this. Pick one day a week when you will skip one of your usual meals—say, lunch on Friday, the usual penitential day for Christians. In the time when you usually would be eating, practice meditation. Give the money you saved to the poor. By meditating you are not fixating on food. By not eating you are helping in this small way all who have nothing to eat.

POINTS FOR FURTHER REFLECTION

1. How do our chosen lifestyle and consumer choices manifest our ethics?

2. How can the greater cultivation of the human virtue of temperance in all things change our usual patterns of consumption of the earth's limited resources?

3. Simone Weil is a witness to fasting in solidarity with the poor. In what ways can she serve or not serve as an example for us?

CHAPTER 6:

The Three Great Pillars of Piety *as* a Practical Program

Fasting and Penance

A proper context for the reevaluation in our time of fasting as a specifically religious practice should take place within the context of the sacrament of penance, which has also suffered a decline in recent times. In this regard Joseph Ratzinger gives us a proper framework by describing penance as a process, not a discrete event.

> Ecclesiastical penance is a process which can and often must continue beyond . . . death. . . . This process points up the difference between someone's valid fundamental decision, whereby he is accepted in grace, and the defective permeation of the effects of that decision throughout

the being of the whole person. . . . [It is] the inwardly necessary process of transformation in which a person becomes capable of Christ, capable of God and thus capable of unity with the whole communion of saints. . . . Man is the recipient of the divine mercy, yet this does not exonerate him from the need to be transformed.[1]

Unlike in ancient times, today sacramental absolution is granted before the completion of the appropriate penance for the transgressions confessed. For the forgiveness of serious sins and reconciliation with the Christian community, the early Church required that the individual join the order of penitents segregated during the eucharistic celebrations and demanded the performance of penance for an extended period. The ancient sequence, it seems, is a superior expression of penance as a process, one that requires hard spiritual work such as the practice of fasting, before absolution is granted.

It was fortuitous that as I was writing this book, Pope Benedict XVI chose as the subject of his Ash Wednesday message for 2009 the restoration in the Church of the practice of fasting as part of what he called "our itinerary of more intense spiritual training." In doing so he made a strict separation between the widespread fixation with dieting and religious fasting.

In our own day, fasting seems to have lost something of its spiritual meaning and has taken on, in a culture characterized by the search for material well-being, a therapeutic value for the care of one's body. Fasting certainly brings benefits to physical well-being, but for believers, it is, in the first place, a "therapy" to heal all that prevents them from conformity to the will of God.

The pope then recalls the two traditional motivations for fasting: to listen to Christ and be fed by his saving word, the hunger and thirst for God; and to open our eyes to the situation in which so many of our brothers and sisters live. Referring to the communal nature of religious fast, he encourages

> the parishes and every other community to intensify in Lent the practice of private and communal fasts, joined to the Word of God, prayer and almsgiving. . . . This practice needs to be rediscovered and encouraged again in our day, especially during the liturgical season of Lent.[2]

May this book be part of this great effort.

A Practical Program for Fasting

As we have seen, in his Ash Wednesday message Pope Benedict makes a clear distinction between fasting as physical therapy and fasting for religious reasons. A fast for physical or medical purposes is defined as "the voluntary abstinence from all food and drink except water, as long as the nutritional reserves of the body are adequate to sustain normal functions." Medical fasting generally serves two goals: internal cleansing and the rejuvenation of the body's systems, and for therapy of a specific disease.[3]

Religious fasting, on the other hand, as I defined it in the preface to this book, is an act of humility before God and a penitential expression of our need for conversion from sin and selfishness to the love of God above all and our neighbor as ourselves. Its aim is the transformation of our total being, mind, body, and spirit. Its necessary companions are prayer and the practice of charity. As we have seen in chapter 1, religious fasting may be total or partial, and the two are undertaken for different purposes. What follows is a suggested program of fasting for the average Christian who does not live in a monastery, but who wishes a more rigorous regime than the minimum prescribed by canon law. In doing this I take as my models and examples the great early practitioners, the desert fathers. In particular I follow in the steps of the formidable St. Anthony of the Desert who, as we have seen, did not right away venture forth into those empty desert spaces for heroic sacrifices of self-denial but first spent time in a hermitage near his village getting ready. Here I propose setting aside time and space at regular intervals throughout the year to engage in specific spiritual and physical practices. In this program, fasting takes place always in conjunction with the practice of the two other pillars, prayer and charitable deeds, the three foundations of Jewish and Christian piety. Their aim is nothing less than complete transformation, the recovery of equilibrium in our daily living, and greater personal freedom in our biological existence. After years of practice of the three pillars, St. Anthony's soul, it was said, could be seen shining right through his body, so unified was he in his total being.

FASTING THROUGHOUT THE YEAR: CREATING A PERSONAL HERMITAGE

Prayer, fasting, and works of charity together are the foundations of our spiritual life. They are such because they engage our total selves — mind, body and spirit — and help us to practice the supreme commandment to love God above all and our neighbor as ourselves. They comprise a correct concept of human nature in all its dignity and glorious destiny, and also an accurate portrayal of its fallen condition and its need for redemption.

Part One: Forging the Link between Fasting and Charity

The practice of charity at the start must be seen not only as an essential accompaniment of our fasting, but as its very goal. We seek through fasting a greater compassion, a softer heart. This is in contrast with a heart that might become more rigid in traditional dieting through mere feats of willpower and self-control. In charity, St. Anthony gave us his personal witness by taking literally the Lord's command to sell all his possessions and give the proceeds to the poor. While that may not be an option for most people, certainly a greater simplicity of life in general and a conscious refusal to buy into the consumerist culture that surrounds us must characterize our piety. To mention just one example, the renting of storage space has become a growth industry in our country because we have acquired so much stuff that even our cluttered garages cannot contain it all anymore. Stepping away into the desert perspective of Lent, we can recognize and repudiate the greed, avarice, and selfish exploitation that pass for normal life in a capitalist society, which bases itself on the profit motive and the accumulation of goods as the only measures of personal success.

A wasteful, throw-away existence is not only characterized by ignorance of the earth's limited resources, but also blinds us to living conditions of the vast populations who earn their living in a globalized market. Poverty of spirit is more important today than ever as a means to practice social charity. In this context we should recall the admonition of the American bishops to strengthen our ascetical practice by designating every Friday not only as a day of penance, but also as a special occasion for the practice of charitable deeds done in the name of Christ. This linkage of penance and charity helps us to keep in mind that divine charity is the perfection we seek through our self-denial. Divine charity may seem like a difficult thing to practice, but a simple act, such as the Skip-a-Meal program described earlier, can give us each week the opportunity to make charitable contributions by spending less on feeding ourselves. If we look, we can find other equally appropriate ways we can incorporate this in our own lives.

This link between self-denial and charity is exemplified in the lives of the early desert ascetics. While solitude was important to these monks, it would be a wrong idea to characterize such ascetics as living lives of total isolation. Such would go against the absolute priority of the practice of charity in ascetical life. Their hermitages often were near villages to whose way of life the hermitage represented constant challenge. There was back and forth constantly between village and hermitage, the people seeking the assistance of the holy man's spiritual power in solving various problems they had and his objectivity and wisdom in tangled human relations. In that society of ultra-patriarchalism, the biological fathers were distant from their children, serving as the awesome preservers of society's strict standards. The holy men took on the function of the warm and loving pedagogue to the youths who came to them for guidance.

Part Two: Prayer and Solitude

The practice of solitude and a daily routine of prayer are key elements if our fasting is to have its desired effects. Only in prayer can we clarify our true life priorities through our conversations with God. St. Anthony withdrew to a hermitage to accomplish this, but at first not far from home. Perhaps for us our hermitage could actually be a space within our home, a favorite chair with a favorite view, a natural scene maybe right outside our window. From this fixed vantage point in the universe, we can contemplate daily the changing seasons and weather, for example, or birds at their feeder, and there have a glimpse of the beauty of God.

Origen, as we have noted, is credited with the development of the form of prayer called *lectio divina*, literally, "divine reading." In the centuries since, this particular way of praying has proved itself to be well suited to our drawing from the riches of the scriptures the spiritual nourishment we seek in solitude. It is, as I hope to show in what follows, a prayer form directly based upon human psychology. It has five steps: (1) the preparation; (2) pondering a chosen text, which can be a single verse or even a single word; (3) imagining yourself being personally addressed by God by it at this moment; (4) making resolutions to apply this message to your life; and finally, (5) resting in the divine presence.

Preparation is necessary before beginning *lectio divina* because, of course, our mind has to be emptied of all else as we enter into the quiet rhythm of contemplation. It is important to make yourself comfortable, to take note of your breathing in and out, and to make use, if it helps, of a favorite mantra. One typical mantra, for example, taken from Russian Orthodox spirituality, is, "Lord Jesus Christ, Son of God, Savior, be merciful to me a sinner." Concentrating on words such as these can help us still our minds so that we are able to truly focus on prayer.

Now we are ready to approach the text. First we use our intellect to discern its literal meaning. We say it over and over to ourselves, pausing to let the words have their impact on us. We ponder what they say, with the help of scripture commentaries if we wish. We think about the context, where this fits within the Bible, and to what the incident or admonition pertains there.

At this point we are ready for liftoff. We rise above the literal text in our imagination. It now is not something from the past, addressed to people long ago, but a living word, not just inspired then but inspiring to me now. I am in the biblical scene. Jesus is talking to me. What is he saying and how does this apply to my present circumstances, the answers I am seeking?

The fourth step engages our will: What do I need to do now in light of what my prayer has disclosed? What changes, what actions must I make in obedience to God's message? I must realize that prayer is never merely "wasting time with Jesus." There is a bottom line to it. My deeper, never-ending conversion is at stake here.

It was at that point that *lectio divina* used to end until, in recent times, its fifth and final step was rediscovered. Sometimes this is called "centering prayer." It is a wordless, thoughtless going to the very center of my being where God resides and resting there in his presence. I am in a state of gracious blessedness, and I pause to enjoy its peace.

Our hermitage solitude sometimes should become extended beyond the usual hour of prayer each day and include a whole day. Very relevant here is the strict observance of the Sabbath rest commanded by God. Letting go of our so-called "urgent" tasks, we can learn humility before God and nurture gratitude for God's gifts.

Part Three: The Examen

While living in the hermitage the solitaries felt it necessary to spend much time in what they called "the weighing of thoughts." During these periods they allowed memories to emerge, some long suppressed, and dream images to be examined. God often speaks to people in their dreams, as we know from the scriptures. Often these memories and dreams have much to tell us about what are called "the seven deadly sins," which actually are not sins but sinful tendencies in ourselves that we need to be aware of. In this regard I think of Buñuel's classic film, *Simon of the Desert*, the life of St. Symeon Stylites, so called because his hermitage was a platform elevated on a pillar (or *stylos* in Greek) where he lived in solitude. From this perch he perceives all kinds of frightening beasts approach, loathsome in appearance. Buñuel's treatment makes it clear that these beasts represent aspects of Symeon himself that he had not previously recognized. This is what an examination of consciousness can help us achieve: recognizing the different aspects of ourselves.

Nowadays "weighing of thoughts" is called an examination of consciousness, which, if done daily, helps us to review each day and its happenings in the light of God. It is an opportunity to seek forgiveness and to set in place good resolutions. Another daily examen is called the "particular examen" in the spirituality taught by St. Ignatius of Loyola. At that time we are to focus on our particular deadly sin, the one we know we are personally inclined to, and strive anew to overcome it by positive action. The reception of the sacrament of reconciliation falls naturally into this "weighing of thoughts" and its grace more fruitfully received.

Part Four: The Fast

Fasting thus finds its appropriate place in this overall regime. As we have seen, throughout the year, early Christians chose Wednesdays and Fridays as days of fasting and abstinence from meat, and we might too. Outside of Lent, our fasting on those days could have as its motivation the repairing of damage done by our sinfulness. Here as we work to develop our own model of fasting, we can refer to the information presented in chapter 1 on the traditions of the Western and Eastern churches, and choose elements that are most appropriate for our own lives.

In crafting our own program, we can also learn from one of the great spiritual masters of the Church, St. Francis de Sales (1567–1622), who offers some helpful observations on fasting, which I summarize below, in his classic *Introduction to the Devout Life*:[4]

1. If you are physically capable of it, set up a routine of fasting on certain days of the week. This will help you control your bodily appetites and grow in virtue, as well as gain your heavenly reward.

2. Practice fasting only with the guidance of a good spiritual director, and always do so with moderation and balance. Francis quotes St. Jerome approvingly: "Immoderate fasts displease me very much."

3. Your work and state in life are primary; fasting should not impede your ability to perform your duties, or endanger your health. Francis states:

One man finds it difficult to fast, another to care for the sick, visit prisoners, hear confessions, preach, comfort the afflicted, pray, and perform similar tasks. These last sufferings are of greater value than the first.

4. Eating what is set before you and not criticizing it, whether you like it or not, is itself a great form of asceticism.

St. Francis was known as an indifferent eater—a contemporary of his tells us that Francis often "paid little or no attention to what he was eating"—but also as a powerful witness to the union of asceticism and social charity. We are told that St. Francis frequently sent uneaten portions of the meals prepared for him to the houses of the poor in his diocese. In this way, while practicing a personal asceticism, he also strove to fulfill the biblical injunction to "be hospitable to one another."

St. Anthony's dwelling for a time in a hermitage near his village, as we have seen, was aimed at preparing himself for the rigors of the vast and open desert where he would spend the rest of his life. In similar fashion, I have recommended that we set up a kind of personal hermitage in our homes to engage faithfully in our religious practices each day. To continue along this line of thought, we should regard the season of Lent each year as our opportunity to go into the desert and intensify and deepen our prayer, fasting, and charity. In this way we, along with the entire Christian community, can make ourselves fit for the new and greater life Easter promises.

Fasting and Good Physical Health

In connection with the practical guide to fasting that I am setting out here, it is perhaps appropriate at this point to say a few words about fasting and physical health, a topic of increasing interest today. More and more, modern medicine aims at treating the person, not just the symptoms the person presents. Greater attention is being given to preventing illness through healthy lifestyles rather than merely handling the recurrent illness that comes from not paying attention to our everyday well-being. The diet-disease linkage, for example, is seen as a key to help the body use its own powers to restore health rather than relying exclusively upon intervention through surgery and medication.

Fostering right eating habits targets directly the growing epidemic of obesity among certain populations and the ill effects of high-fat, highly refined food products. In this reevaluation, fasting is being given a new look as a means to allow the body to rest, recover its energy, and expel toxins. The daily diet recommended by Dr. Joel Fuhrman in his book, *Fasting and Eating for Health*, de-emphasizes meat, chicken, fish, and dairy products, and recommends the total avoidance of all processed foods, fried food, fats, and sweets.[5] This clearly parallels the dietary regulations of Christian ascetical practices, suggesting that these practices are beneficial to the body as well as to the spirit.

During a parish retreat that I was giving, I met a man who told me, with some pride as well as humility, about a medically supervised fast that he had successfully undertaken. Our conversations were prompted by a conference I gave during the retreat about the religious necessity and benefits of fasting. Moving into middle age, and in reasonably good health, he shared with a coworker his long-held desire to engage in a program of fasting to improve the overall quality of his life. She encouraged him to begin and proved a constant source of support during the entire period of the fast. He lost eighty-four pounds in eighty-four days. Along with his family at home, who did not participate in the fast, his co-worker helped him achieve his targets all along the way, which proved to be easier, not more difficult, as time went on.

Under the supervision of his physician, he started the pre-fast phase: during this period he ate a leafy salad as his exclusive evening meal. Then he advanced to a juice phase, and in the final phase relied mostly on vegetable broths for nourishment. As the weeks of his fast unfolded, he said he experienced a growing "crescendo" of benefits. He had energy to burn, for one thing. On the basketball court he found he could out-pass other players twenty years younger than himself. His ability to hear and see became sharper, more vivid. By a kind of "knowing" without being able to say precisely how, he felt his total health to be the best in years.

There were of course difficulties along the way. Eating is a human activity that is profoundly social: just watch a person eating alone in a restaurant and you immediately recognize how eating means much more than refueling. It was hard for him to get out for dinner with family and friends, as people often do, and then have to watch them eat while he sipped tea all evening. The support he was given by his family and friends, however, proved to be crucial in helping him stay the course. Another problem emerged later, when the fast was over. He then found it harder, not easier, to lose more weight, because his body had become accustomed to storing up nutrition from his smaller portions to ensure survival.

Nevertheless, the beneficial effects of the fast in general continue, as he has been able to successfully maintain his weight loss and health.

Others have written about their experience of such medical fasts and attest that the greatest benefit was that the fast helped them maintain good health as a priority in their lives. They tend to pay more attention to the "numbers": blood pressure, cholesterol, blood sugars, and triglycerides. They make sure they fit regular exercise time into their daily schedule. They have discovered the wisdom of the advice with which Michael Pollan summarizes the message of his book, *The Omnivore's Dilemma*: eat slowly, eat less, eat food (that is, something your grandmother would recognize as food, something non-processed), and eat mostly leaves.

Margaret Miles, in the book already cited, mentions another benefit which comes from altering the usual pattern of our days by regular fasts. Who says we must follow an iron-clad regimen of three meals a day? Fasting gives us new freedom not only from the tyranny of bodily cravings, but also through a new sense of time and how we organize it. Through the practice of fasting on a regular basis it begins to dawn on us how much in the past our lives and our individual days have been structured around food. We seem constantly to be planning meals, shopping for food, preparing it, eating it, and cleaning up afterward. Miles makes this observation:

> Altering our eating patterns, even briefly, both teaches us the depth of our attachment to food and to mealtimes and loosens our attachment so that it never again has quite the strength that it had when we were not conscious of it.[6]

Finally, with regard to fasting and bodily health, it is significant that the early ascetics, including Anthony himself, did not live sedentary or slothful existences in their hermitages. Anthony limited his sleep and engaged in strenuous manual labor. For us as well, in combination with our fasting, changing our sleeping patterns to engage in prayer during the night and doing regular physical exercise can be good ways to engage and heal our body and spirit together.

Other Forms of Fasting

The object of our fast, however, need not be limited to food and drink. Pope Benedict XVI has urged us to fast from noise, and from the media in particular, during Lent. We could also profitably abstain from useless conversation and recreations, and spend the time in spiritual reading.

In his book *A Time To Keep Silence*, Patrick Leigh Fermor describes his experiences living for extended periods of time in various monasteries in France. His original intention was merely to find an inexpensive place to live while he did some writing. What happened to him completely unexpectedly, he says, was that this exposure to a totally different way of life resulted in an extraordinary personal transformation. What completely changed him and made him realize how abnormal his life had been until then was the silence. In his words,

> The explanation is simple enough: the desire for talk, movement and nervous expression that I had transported from Paris found, in this silent place, no response or foil, evoked no single echo; after miserably gesticulating for a while in a vacuum, it languished and finally died for lack of any stimulus or nourishment. Then the

tremendous accumulation of tiredness, which must be the common property of all our contemporaries, broke loose and swamped everything. No demands, once I had emerged from the flood of sleep, were made upon my nervous energy: there were no automatic drains, such as conversation at meals, small talk, catching trains, or the hundred anxious trivialities that poison everyday life. Even the major causes of guilt and anxiety had slid away into some distinct limbo and not only failed to emerge in the small hours as tormentors but appeared to have lost their dragonish validity. This new dispensation left nineteen hours a day of absolute and god-like freedom.[7]

Here, reproduced on a much smaller scale, was replicated the experience of the desert fathers: a new perspective on the toxic aspects of life in the world, a newly discovered capacity to expel these toxins, and the amazing knowledge of personal freedom.

Early in his stay in one of these monasteries, he engaged in a conversation with the abbot and confided what a "blessed relief" it was not to be talking all the time. To this the abbot replied, "Yes, it is marvelous. In the world outside our walls, there is a great abuse of words."[8] These words were spoken fifty years ago, before the arrival of mobile phones, iPods, and BlackBerries. How much more toxic the atmosphere has become and, sadly, how little we realize it.

Working on our anger and striving to gain more self-control are also related to fasting. Avoiding the complaint mentality and consciously adopting a grateful attitude toward our life would be for many a true change of heart. A judgmental attitude poisons our human relationships and we need to "fast" from it the best we can. The pursuit of greater simplicity of life, resistance to the consumer mentality, and greater capacity to distinguish our needs from our wants are also part of fasting broadly conceived.

A distinctive feature of fasting in the Byzantine tradition is a conscious curtailment of entertainment. The four fasting seasons are considered "closed time" in which even the celebration of marriage is considered inappropriate. In many homes, musical instruments are put aside for the full period of Lent, and, in more observant homes, the enjoyment of radio and television is greatly reduced, if not eliminated. These customs seek to reinforce the opportunity for greater prayer and recollection during fasting times.

POINTS FOR FURTHER REFLECTION

1. If you are a Catholic of the Roman or Byzantine rite and wish to begin a more rigorous program of fasting as outlined above, what practices would you put in place throughout the year?

2. During the Lenten season how do you imagine yourself intensifying the practice of the three pillars?

3. Reflect on your own prayer experiences until now. How might you deepen these experiences?

Fasting *and* Feasting: The Spirituality *of* Fasting

In the Gospel According to St. Mark, Jesus responds to the disappointment of the disciples that they had been unable to dispel a demon by saying, "This is the kind that can be driven out only by prayer" (Mk 9:29). To this saying of Jesus there is a variant reading given in some ancient texts, "This kind cannot be driven out by anything but prayer and fasting." Did the disappointing experience of the first Christians in trying to drive out demons by prayer alone cause such an important addition to be made to Jesus' words? And was it the awareness of the sad decline in fasting among contemporary Catholics that prompted Pope Benedict XVI, in his book of Lenten reflections, *Journey to Easter*, to cite this same saying in its expanded version?[1] Whatever the reason, then and now, the practice of fasting remains not only a healthy practice for living, but a pillar of faith. As the desert fathers already knew, faith always must come down to body level if it is real.

Cardinal John Henry Newman (1801–90), the venerable Victorian churchman and convert to Catholicism, during his Anglican years delivered a homily which he entitled, "The Cross of Christ, the Measure of the World." His words are a fitting insight into the spiritual meaning of fasting within the context of the cross of Christ.

The homily begins with allusion to the common human task of trying to make sense of and interpret the world into which we have been born. How are we to look at things? What is the real key, the right understanding of life? For Christians, Newman claims, it must be the cross of Christ. This view, he concedes, is not obvious. A more superficial account would find the cross to be an obstacle, something that prevents us from enjoying the world; on this account, Newman says, the "doctrine of the Cross, it may be said, disarranges two parts of the system which seem made for each other, the enjoyment from the enjoyer." This, Newman reminds us, is precisely what Eve came to believe, at Satan's instigation, about God's prohibition about eating the forbidden fruit. But according to the wisdom of the Cross, that "great and awful doctrine," the very heart of the Christian religion, things are not so simple. The Cross in fact is not about embracing sadness and the deprivation of pleasure, but rather how actually to achieve joy and happiness. Newman explains:

> The Cross will lead us to mourning, repentance, humiliation, prayer, fasting; we shall sorrow for our sins,

we shall sorrow with Christ's sufferings; but all this sorrow will only issue, nay, will be undergone in a happiness far greater than the enjoyment which the world gives, though careless worldly minds indeed will not believe this, ridicule the notion of it, because they have never tasted it.

Newman's homily concludes with these soaring sentences:

Let us "seek first the Kingdom of God and his righteousness" and then all those things of the world "will be added to us." They alone are truly able to enjoy this world who begin with the world unseen. They alone enjoy it, who have first abstained from it. They alone can truly feast, who have first fasted; they alone are able to use the world who have learned not to abuse it; they alone inherit it, who take it as a shadow of the world to come, and who for that world to come relinquish it.[2]

In the Catholicism of Newman's period, the cross was indeed the focus of religious life. In more recent times, the churches of East and West have seen the cross and the glorious resurrection as part of the one great paschal mystery, Christ's passage from death to life. This is where even in our earthly existence there is place not just for fasting but for feasting. There are, for example, among the Slavic peoples, the traditions not just of fasting but of breaking the fast. Special blessings are conferred upon the rich and lavish paschal foods, blessings that speak of God giving back to us in abundance all the good things we have freely given up. We fast not just for fasting's sake, but to be able to feast, to live even in the present with great pleasure and a joy that lasts.

It is appropriate in a book on the Christian practice of fasting to end with feasting. As we have seen, Christian fasting is not based upon a distaste for food as such, as a dangerous luxury, or upon a hatred of our bodily selves and self-punishment. We fast to feast. Regarding the basic human act of eating as a thoughtless refueling exercise is to demean human life and to deprive us of its pleasure. At this point I look not to a theologian but to a food writer, M. F. K. Fisher, author of the classic work *The Art of Eating*. In it she writes:

> The ability to choose what food you must eat, and knowingly, will make you able to choose other less transitory things with courage and finesse. A child should be encouraged, not discouraged, as so many are, to look at what he eats, and think about it: the juxtapositions of color and flavor and texture . . . and indirectly the reasons why he is eating it and the results it will have on him, if he is an introspective widgin.[3]

To put it another way, the human act of eating, if it is truly human, is a conscious one: we choose what we eat, and we appreciate it with thanksgiving. Jesus chose to commemorate himself in a meal which later Christians would call *agape*, "love," for food draws us together. If you have ever eaten alone in a restaurant, you know how unnatural an experience this is. This commemorative feast of love is also called eucharist, "giving thanks," because the act of eating opens us up to the God who opens his hands and fills all his creatures with good things.

It is not at all inappropriate, therefore, for our future life of the resurrection to be depicted as a heavenly banquet where the food is plentiful (Jn 6:13) and the wine inexhaustible and of the finest vintage (Jn 2:10). This is the return to Paradise that Christ made possible.

Notes

Preface

1. Alexander Schmemann, *Great Lent: Journey to Pascha* (New York: St. Vladimir's Seminary, 1969).

Introduction

1. Pope Paul VI, *Apostolic Constitution on Fast and Abstinence* (*Poenitemini*), February 17, 1966, trans. National Catholic Welfare Conference, Washington, D.C.

2. Second Vatican Council, *The Decree on Priestly Formation* (*Optatum totius*), no. 16, in *The Documents of Vatican II*, ed. Walter M. Abbot, S.J. (New York: Crossroad, 1989).

3. *Catechism of the Catholic Church,* Second Edition (Vatican City: Libreria Editrice Vaticana, 2000), n. 1434.

4. Second Vatican Council, *Dogmatic Constitution on the Church (Lumen gentium)*, nos. 40–41 in *The Documents of Vatican II*, ed. Abbott.

5. Karen Armstrong, introduction to *A Time to Keep Silence* by Patrick Leigh Fermor, (New York: *New York Review of Books*, 2007), xiii–xiv.

6. Michael Pollan, *The Omnivore's Dilemma: A Natural History of Four Meals* (New York: Penguin, 2006), 2.

7. Aelred Squire, *Asking the Fathers* (New York: Morehouse-Barlow, 1973), 57.

8. Video message on the Keith Urban website, http://www.keithurban.net/site.php.

9. Joseph Ratzinger, *Journey to Easter: Spiritual Reflections for the Season of Lent* (New York: Crossroad, 1987), 23–24.

CHAPTER 1: REDISCOVERING A TRADITION

1. Joseph I. Dirvin, C.M., *Mrs. Seton: Foundress of the American Sisters of Charity* (New York: Farrar, Straus and Cudahy, 1962), 138.

2. Gregory Dix, *The Shape of the Liturgy* (London: Dacre, 1943), 354–55.

3. J. A. Jungmann, S.J., *Pastoral Liturgy* (New York: Herder and Herder, 1962), 227.

4. Thomas Aquinas, *Summa Theologiae*, Ia IIae, Q 147, trans. Thomas Gilby, O.P. (New York: McGraw-Hill, 1964), vol. 43.

5. Ibid.

6. Schmemann, *Great Lent*, 49, 97–98.

7. Ibid., 43.

8. United States Conference of Catholic Bishops, Committee on Divine Worship, *Newsletter*, December, 2003.

9. United States Conference of Catholic Bishops, "Pastoral Statement on Penance and Abstinence," November 18, 1966.

10. Paul VI and Shenouda III, "Common Declaration of Pope Paul VI and of the Pope of Alexandria Shenouda III," the Vatican, May 10, 1973.

CHAPTER 2: A BODY HUMBLE BEFORE GOD

1. W. D. Davies, *The Setting of the Sermon on the Mount* (Cambridge: Cambridge University Press, 1966), 96.

2. Robert J. Karris, O.F.M., "The Gospel According to St. Luke," in *The Jerome Biblical Commentary*, ed. Raymond E. Brown, S.S., Joseph A. Fitzmyer, S.J., and Roland E. Murphy, O.Carm. (Englewood Cliffs, N.J.: Prentice Hall, 1990), 688.

3. M. Viller, founding ed., *Dictionnaire de spiritualité ascetique et mystique, doctrine et histoire*, vol. 8 (Paris: Beauchesne, 1974), 1174 (translation by the author).

CHAPTER 3: A BODY FIT FOR RESURRECTION

1. Henri Couzel, *Origen*, trans. A. B. Worral (San Francisco: Harper and Row, 1989), 11.

2. Cited in G. M. A. Grube, *Plato's Thought* (Indianapolis: Hackett, 1980), 125.

3. Peter Brown, *The Body and Society* (New York: Columbia University Press, 2008), 220–21.

4. Ibid., 164.

5. Ibid., 167.

6. John D. Zizioulas, *Being as Communion* (Crestwood, N.Y.: St. Vladimir's Seminary Press, 1985), 52.

7. William Harmless, S.J., *Desert Christians* (New York: Oxford University Press, 2004), 312.

8. Columba Stewart, *Cassian the Monk* (New York: Oxford University Press, 1998), 50.

9. *De institutis* 5,14.4. Cited in Harmless, *Desert Christians*, 345.

10. Stewart, *Cassian the Monk*, 63.

11. Brown, *The Body and Society*, 237.

12. Ibid., 225.

Chapter 4: A Body Beatifully Made

1. Augustine, *The Confessions of St. Augustine*, bk. 11, ch. 4, no. 6, trans. John K. Ryan (New York: Doubleday Image, 1960), 280.

2. Augustine, *The Confessions*, 70.

3. Ibid., 189.

4. Augustine, *The Confessions*, V11, 11, cited in Margaret R. Miles, *Fullness of Life: Historical Foundations for a New Asceticism* (Philadelphia: Westminster, 1981), 67.

5. Augustine, *De libero arbitrio*, II, XVI, 41. Cited in Miles, *Fullness of Life*, 67.

6. Miles, *Fullness of Life*, 68.

7. Gerald A. McCool, ed., *A Rahner Reader* (New York: Crossroad, 1975), 200, 202.

8. Miles, *Fullness of Life*, 16.

9. Kate Zerniki, "My Not-Even-Remotely Funny Valentine," *New York Times*, Sunday edition, February 11, 2007, Section 4.3.

10. Augustine, *Anti-Pelagian Writings: A Select Library of the Nicene and Post-Nicene Fathers of the Christian Church*, vol. 5 (Grand Rapids, Mich.: Eerdmans, 1961), 164.

11. Jerome Murphy-O'Connor, O.P., "The First Letter to the Corinthians," in *The New Jerome Biblical Commentary*, ed. Brown, Fitzmyer, Murphy, 803.

12. Caroline Walker Bynum, *Holy Fast and Holy Feast: The Religious Significance of Food for Medieval Women* (Berkeley: University of California Press, 1987), 294.

13. John Paul II, *Original Unity of Man and Woman: Catechesis on the Book of Genesis* (Boston: Daughters of St. Paul, 1981), 54, 57.

14. Ibid., 77, no. 2.

15. Joseph Ratzinger, *Eschatology: Death and Eternal Life* (Washington, D.C.: Catholic University of America Press, 1988), 149, 179.

16. Pope Benedict XVI, *Deus caritas est* (Vatican City: Libreria Editrice Vaticana), no. 5.

Chapter 5: A Body Socially Responsible

1. Augustine, discourse on Psalm 42, section 8. Cited in Thomas Ryan, C.S.P., *The Sacred Art of Fasting: Preparing to Practice* (Woodstock, N.Y.: Skylight Paths, 2005), 46–47.

2. *Didache* 1.3. Cited in Brown, *The Body and Society*, 43.

3. Walker Bynum, *Holy Fast and Holy Feast*, 220.

4. Pope Benedict XVI, *Deus caritas est*, nos. 19–20.

5. John E. Carroll, *The Wisdom of Small Farms and Local Food: Aldo Leopold's Land Ethic and Sustainable Agriculture* (Durham: University of New Hampshire Press, 2005), 10–11.

6. See *Compendium of the Social Doctrine of the Church* (Vatican City: Libreria Editrice Vaticana, 2004), nos. 171–84.

7. Pope John Paul II, *Sollicitudo rei socialis*, No. 28. Cited in *Compendium of the Social Doctrine of the Church*, 253.

8. M. T. Anderson, *Feed* (Cambridge, Mass.: Candlewick, 2002), 110.

9. Ibid., 290.

10. Josef Pieper, *The Four Cardinal Virtues* (Notre Dame: University of Notre Dame Press, 1967), 146–47.

11. Ibid., 182.

12. Simone Weil, *Waiting for God*, trans. Emma Craufurd (New York: Harper and Row, 1951), 66.

13. George Steiner, "Bad Friday," *New Yorker*, March 2, 1992, 86.

14. J. M. Cameron, "The Life and Death of Simone Weil," *New York Review of Books*, March 3, 1977, 7.

15. Thomas R. Nevin, *Simone Weil: Portrait of a Self-Exiled Jew* (Chapel Hill: University of North Carolina, 1991), 386, xii.

16. Elizabeth Hardwick, *New York Times Book Review*, January 23, 1977, 1.

17. Simone Petremont, *Simone Weil: A Life* (New York: Pantheon, 1976), 51.

18. Ibid., 330.

19. Steiner, "Bad Friday," 91.

20. Robert Coles, *Simone Weil: A Modern Pilgrimage* (Woodstock: Skylight Paths, 2001), 41.

21. Vernon Sproxton, "Pilgrim of the Absolute," in *Simone Weil: Gateway to God*, ed. David Raper (Glasgow: William Collins Sons, 1974), 29.

22. Personal letter, April 22, 2007.

23. *Catholic News*, Singapore, Sunday, July 22, 2007, vol. 57, no. 15, 4.

CHAPTER 6: THE THREE GREAT PILLARS OF PIETY AS A PRACTICAL PROGRAM

1. Ratzinger, *Eschatology*, 230–31.

2. *L'Osservatore Romano*, weekly English edition, Wednesday, February 11, 2009, no. 6, 2081.6.

3. Joel Fuhrman, M.D., *Fasting and Eating for Health: A Medical Doctor's Program for Conquering Disease* (New York: St. Martin's, 1995), 8, 24.

4. Francis de Sales, *Introduction to the Devout Life*, trans. and ed. John K. Ryan (New York: Doubleday, 1989), 185–86. See also my treatment of St. Francis's spirituality in

Belonging to God: A Personal Training Guide for the Deeper Catholic Spiritual Life (New York: Crossroad, 2004), particularly pp. 139–151 on eating and the spiritual life.

5. Furhman, *Fasting and Eating for Health*, 25–26.

6. Miles, *Fullness of Life*, 160.

7. Patrick Leigh Fermor, *A Time To Keep Silence* (New York: New York Review of Books, 2007), 23.

8. Ibid., 38.

CONCLUSION

1. Ratzinger, *Journey to Easter*, 23.

2. John Henry Newman, *Parochial and Plain Sermons* (San Francisco: Ignatius Press, 1987), 1234–35.

3. M. F. K. Fisher, *The Art of Eating* (New York: MacMillan, 1990), 321.

Monsignor Charles M. Murphy is currently the Director of the Permanent Diaconate for the Diocese of Portland (Maine). He is the author of a number of scholarly articles as well as several books, including *At Home on the Earth: Foundations for a Catholic Ethics of the Environment*, (Crossroad, 1989), *Wallace Stevens: A Spiritual Poet in a Secular Age* (Paulist, 1997), and *Belonging to God: A Personal Training Guide for the Deeper Catholic Spiritual Life* (Crossroad, 2004). Msgr. Murphy is the former Academic Dean and Rector of the Pontifical North American College, Vatican City, and he served as part of the editorial group working in Italy under Cardinal Ratzinger on the third draft of the *Catechism of the Catholic Church*, which became the fourth and final version. He is currently a consultant to the USCCB committee on catechetics, reviewing materials for conformity with the Catechism. Msgr. Murphy served as chair of the editorial committee which produced the pastoral letter on environmental issues by the Bishops of the Boston Province and he served as a consultant to the USCCB for their statement on global warming. He has been the pastor of four parishes in Maine: Sacred Heart, Yarmouth; St. Mary's, Westbrook; St. Pius X, Portland; and Holy Martyrs, Falmouth. In addition he has served his diocese as ecumenical officer, Director of Education (Catholic schools and religious education), and Director of the Diaconate, his present position. Msgr. Murphy holds a Doctorate in Sacred Theology from the Gregorian University in Rome (1982), a Master's degree in Education from Harvard University (1958), and an A.B. in Classics from the College of the Holy Cross (1957).

Founded in 1865, Ave Maria Press,
a ministry of the Congregation of
Holy Cross, is a Catholic publishing
company that serves the spiritual and
formative needs of the Church and its
schools, institutions, and ministers;
Christian individuals and families; and
others seeking spiritual nourishment.

For a complete listing of titles from

Ave Maria Press

Sorin Books

Forest of Peace

Christian Classics

visit www.avemariapress.com

 ave maria press / Notre Dame, IN 46556
A Ministry of the Indiana Province of Holy Cross